How to TEXT WOMEN

Why Chasing Doesn't Work, And You Should Actually Do Less.

*The Unexpected Strategy For Men To Stop Getting Ghosted
And Be The Man Women Respect, Desire,
And Want To Be With*

Includes real-world text interactions for hands-on learning

JESSE TYLER

DISCLAIMER:

This book is intended for educational purposes only. The information contained in this book is provided "as is" and without warranties of any kind, either express or implied.

Please be mindful of the individual boundaries and preferences of the women you are communicating with, and always obtain their explicit consent before pursuing any form of communication or relationship. The examples contained in this book are for illustrative purposes only and are not intended to represent or guarantee that anyone will achieve similar results. Your results may vary and depend on various factors, including but not limited to your background, experience, and individual efforts. This book is not intended for distribution to, or use by, any person or entity in any jurisdiction or country where such distribution or use would be contrary to local law or regulation.

This is my gift to you. I want you to take control of your life and your relationships with women, and I'm here to help you to the best of my knowledge to put you in the driver seat. You need to be aware of these things so you can create the dating life you truly want

♂

masterthedynamic.com

TABLE OF CONTENTS

INTRODUCTION

Over the last 20 years, dating has changed significantly, and how people meet and connect with potential partners has evolved with technology and social trends. Modern dating is all we have now and will never return to what it was before the internet. Being or not in a relationship, you will be talking to women via text most of the time.

There is something that most men don't think about and need to be aware of. When it comes to texting women and generating attraction: Less is more. Most men are just doing too much and not getting anywhere. They think they always need to be doing something, for example:

- Using silly pickup lines
- Constantly checking up on her
- Sending her the good morning and good night texts
- Validating her
- Being the nice guy
- Chasing her

They seem to think that the more they are in her face, the more she'll notice them. Well no. In reality, most men are over-pursuing and talking/texting the girl out of liking them. We dig our graves and don't even realize we are doing it. This is not about doing anything, being an asshole, or boring. Doing less of something doesn't mean doing anything. It is about understanding the game, not overdoing and, at the same time, taking the right actions. Instead of trying constantly seeking attention or reassurance from the woman, it is often better to be more independent and self-reliant. This can involve maintaining your own interests and activities and not letting your interactions with the woman you are texting become the main focus of your life. By being more independent and self-reliant, you can often make a better impression on the woman and create a more balanced and healthy relationship. You want to get compliance with women, and you are not going to get that by chasing them.

We will be talking about how guys fall into an illusion of action. "I need to do something." Does this feeling sound familiar to you? This feeling makes men go over the top when texting women and blowing up their phones, which doesn't work to get them to like you. Chasing doesn't work, and needy behaviors like this are what is getting you ghosted and rejected in the first place. What you will learn first is that whatever your efforts are if you are overdoing them, you need to cut them in half and combine that with the right actions; this will double your results, and if your texting skills improve, your dating life will improve. This book will teach you how to text women effectively, common mistakes men make when texting, why it is so hard to date as a man these days, the difference between chasing and pursuing, the game from a female perspective, and many other things to improve your texting skills and with that your dating life. We will include real text conversations as examples, which are changed slightly for copyright reasons. But we will maintain the interaction's general idea. Self-awareness is an important quality for men to have in order to be successful with women. Having a strong self-awareness allows men to understand their thoughts, feelings, and motivations and how these factors influence their interactions with women. This can help you understand your behavior's impact on women and adjust their behavior in response to feedback and criticism. I hope you find this book valuable and gives you the foundations you need to succeed. Texting is a powerful communication and connection tool; by learning how to use it effectively, you can create more enjoyable and fulfilling relationships with women. This can lead to more enjoyable and rewarding experiences in your dating life. Awareness brings insight, insight brings knowledge, and, combined with action, creates change. I hope this book will help you achieve that.

CHAPTER 1

LESS IS MORE WITH WOMEN

*"Women Are More Attracted to Men
Whose Feelings Are Unclear"*

Study published by the
Association for Psychological Science, *February 2011*

You are texting her a lot. You are trying to catch her attention and get her to notice you, sending good morning and good night texts, checking up on her in the middle of the day, and thinking about the best way for her to notice you and get her attention. You try to get creative by sending her random and silly pickup lines. You subconsciously think that the best strategy is being in her face all the time so that she will notice you over all these other guys who are also blowing up her phone, so you can stand out because you are the one doing it the most. Many guys do this, and when they are not receiving the response they were expecting, they start pursuing and chasing the girl even more until she eventually completely vanishes away. And this leaves you confused; you ask yourself what happened.

You don't understand why you always get rejected and what in the world you need to do to get these girls to like you. This is what happened: You talked these girls out of liking you, you probably showed yourself a bit desperate, came off as low value, and turned the girl off. The first thing you have to do is to stop blowing up her phone.

The frequency of your texts needs to be lower. Nice guys who don't have anything going on for themselves are guilty of this mistake. And I cannot blame you for this entirely. We grew up watching these romantic movies where the guy who gets the girl is the guy that has been pushing and chasing the most-showing at her place with flowers, sending love letters, and all that fairytale. And I am here to tell you that is complete bullshit. With modern dating, talking and texting too much, going on too many dates too soon, and over-pursuing will cause the women to back off and lose interest in you. Most guys are unaware that with women, one thing is what they say they want, and another is what they respond to and get aroused by. When you are texting a woman too much, especially at the beginning, you make her get too familiar with you, she starts feeling confident about herself with you, and she gets bored of you because you are not a challenge.

A woman has been with enough high-value men to know how they act. High-value men are not doing any of this. When you are over-pursuing her by constantly texting her all the time, trying to get her attention, she doesn't perceive you as a high-value man who has a life and is just interested in her; she perceives you as a low-value man that is too desperate and probably doesn't have much success with women. Texting a girl less makes you appear more confident, busy, and secure. You are not chasing her, which makes you not disadvantaged in the interaction. You are more mysterious, and those traits are attractive to women. Women are used to beta male orbiters, and most of the time, they are repulsed by them; they use them only for validation and free attention, and they will never consider them as a sexual partner, let alone a relationship. It is not attractive to a woman when you are all over her, chasing her all the time. The best scenario in a relationship and how it typically works best is when she is chasing your validation. Not the other way around. Especially at the beginning, your job when texting is to build her investment over time, not to get to know each other. Avoid a lot of small talks and use the phone mainly to set up a date. Coming off too strong by chasing her will get you friend-zoned or ghosted. If you see that she is not putting in the same level of effort or investment as you are, you need to stop trying so hard and match her level of investment. Get a life, and get busy working on your goals. Text her and forget. Do not make this woman you are texting the center of your life. Overpersuing doesn't work, and chasing definitely doesn't work with women. When you are texting her less and getting her to invest slowly over time, it is a more natural way for her attraction to grow towards you. Do not tell her everything about yourself too soon, be a bit of a mystery; when you text too much before meeting, there are not many topics for conversation on the date, making it awkward. When you mirror her investment level, you don't have to worry about coming off needy or clingy. You don't have to think about creative pickup lines, which lowers the burden on your end.

Women are attracted to guys who are not always available, with goals, and guys who have a life and are working on something. Avoid giving too much validation at the beginning. Make her earn your validation by her investing more in the conversation. By not being like every other guy simping for her. Most guys talk the girl out of liking them by over-texting, overinvesting, and proving themselves to them. And trust me, women can see this. She needs to see you as more of a catch or a challenge instead and cannot take you for granted. People gravitate towards things perceived as high value, and women are no different. She needs to see you as a guy with an exciting and fulfilling life, and it is not all day by his phone waiting for her to text him back. This doesn't mean to be boring and text her one-word answers. We will get into the details of how to flow a conversation in a way that makes you seem like a high-value man, being attractive, pursuing, and persisting without being the typical needy guy that turns her off. When getting to know a girl, you need to use the phone mainly to set up a date. You need to save meaningful conversations when you are on a date with her, do not talk about yourself a lot and keep it more about her. All you will do with excessive action is kill the attraction. Keep conversations short, engaging, flirty, and mysterious. The goal you want is to have a high perceived value. If she perceives you as a

high-value man, it would be easier to text her than if she doesn't perceive you as such. And it depends on your behavior and your texting style with her.

The Illusion of Action.

<u>You Are Trying Too Hard</u>

There is an illusion of action that most guys have; this illusion makes you over-invest and text more than you should because you believe you need to do more. Some possible reasons include wanting to feel connected to the woman, trying to impress her, or wanting to keep the conversation going. It is also possible that the man might not realize that he is over texting or that he is doing it because he is anxious or unsure of how to communicate effectively.

This makes you seem needy or clingy in your text interactions with women; you come across as insecure and unconfident, which is not attractive to most people. Additionally, it can make the other person feel suffocated and overwhelmed, which is likely to push them away rather than draw them closer to you. Furthermore, being needy or clingy can be a major turn-off to women and lowers your perceived value. Ultimately, it's important to be yourself and communicate naturally and authentically. But at the same time, be aware of what you are doing wrong. When a woman's investment is low, you don't have to chase; you have to build it over time

You can keep conversations interesting without over-investing. As you see from this example, he is keeping the same level of energy and investment as her but at the same time flowing with the conversation and keeping it exciting and engaging. At the beginning of your interaction with a woman, your job is not to sell and prove yourself to her. Your job is to get her to invest more in the conversation by being flirty, interesting, and not overly wordy. Enough for you to get compliance when you ask her to meet with you. Once you build some investment, you must move to the meetup. Hold off a bit with all the long paragraphs, the validation, and compliments. Leave that more when you have a serious relationship with her. She needs to earn your validation by showing compliance and investing in the conversation. Do not just give it away.

Create the vibe that you have a life, that you are a busy man and that you are indifferent if she is interested in you or not. Have a little bit of a take it or leave it attitude. Being in a no-hungry state and having an abundance mindset makes you attractive in a woman's eyes, which will get her to develop an attraction for you.

You only need to increase your perceived value and get her to slowly and progressively invest more in the conversation until you effectively get her to meet up with you.

It is unnecessary to give everything you feel and think and put it into a text. If you are always the one that's initiating and pushing the conversation, you are not giving her any space to chase you. Lower the attention-seeking behavior and mirror her investment.

You want to keep your text within the same investment amount as hers. She hasn't earned so much attention from you yet, and she knows that. You don't have to be her dancing monkey; Mirror her response time as well. Do not text her back right away every single time. A common mistake many guys make is that when a woman texts them, they stop whatever they are doing and text her back right away. Keep doing what you are doing and text her later when you have time or feel like it. Unless you are sexting her or she responds to you immediately, you want to keep that momentum. Still, those are just the exceptions and typically happen later in the relationship with the girl and not so much at the beginning of the interaction. Do not think that if you don't respond right away, she will lose interest or forget about you. Most of the time, the exact opposite is true. If you are too available, then that is when she takes you for granted, loses interest, or forgets about you. If you are not so available, your texts are more valuable, and you will get her to wonder why you are not texting her back, and she will sense that you have a life and that you are not all over her. These types of behavior get a woman's mind racing. I want to make something clear. THIS DOES NOT MEAN YOU ARE NOT SUPPOSED TO INITIATE THE CONVERSATION EVER. In the beginning, especially is when you will almost always have to initiate the conversation. Still, once you start building some investment, maybe you had a couple of dates when her, do not always initiate. Give her time and space for her to do it sometimes as well.

When it comes to social media. Please avoid liking all of her pictures or stories. Do not chase her online by commenting on every picture or responding to every comment she posts. Women usually date men who are doing none of that. The mystery and the wondering will help you with her, and you will instantly be more attractive to her. Most dudes are blowing up their phone, validating her, complimenting her, texting her right away, and double, triple, or quadruple texting her without even getting a reply back, and many of them keep going it is incredible how many simps are there and how they keep doing more of what doesnt work.

It is sad the number of men out there that have no standards, no backbone whatsoever, and they simp for a woman like this with the hope that one day she will give them a chance. Keep yourself together and get straight to the point. The purpose of texting is not to have long conversations. Leave that when you meet her in person. The purpose of texting is mainly to get her to meet up with you. It doesnt mean that you have to only talk to her to ask her out, but you keep the conversations just good enough to keep her on track for a meetup. Many guys make the mistake of talking about their whole lives thru text, have all kinds of conversations, and by the time they meet up (If they even get to that point), the date is a little awkward because you already had a lot of conversations thru text. Do not be her texting buddy. Have some conversation that's fine but move it to the meetup sooner than later, and we will go later in the book about how to ask the women out correctly.

We will learn how to ask her out properly by following a process in chapter 4, *"How to ask her out and close."*

The Difference Between

<u>**Chasing and Persuing**</u>

Chasing and pursuing a woman are two completely different things. You need to know the difference between them and why you never ever want to chase. When you are chasing something, or someone is usually one-sided, it means that it is running away from you, and it doesnt want to be caught. You are seeking her attention and validation, you are the one after her, and it is not being reciprocated. Chasing often connotes a sense of desperation or urgency, as if the man is frantically trying to catch up with the woman and win her over. It can also imply that the man is willing to go to great lengths or make significant sacrifices to win the woman's affection. You are going out of your way to win her over by doing extra stuff when in reality, it is turning her off and making her look down on you. Some examples of chasing are

- Constantly text or call a woman, even if she is not responding or interested.
- Making grand gestures or promises in an effort to win a woman's affection.
- Following a woman around or showing up uninvited in an attempt to get her attention.

- Going to great lengths or making significant sacrifices in order to impress a woman.
- Being overly eager to please a woman and do things for her without expecting anything in return.
- Being excessively jealous or possessive in an effort to keep a woman's attention

These behaviors can be seen as chasing because they suggest that the man is desperate for the woman's attention and is willing to go to great lengths to win her over. They can also be seen as lacking in self-respect, as the man is not setting boundaries for himself and is not valuing his own needs and wants. In general, chasing behavior is not typically seen as attractive or desirable and may even push the woman away rather than draw her closer. On the flip side, pursuing looks a lot different. Someone who is pursuing is able to walk away, you are showing interest, but you are patient and being ok regardless of the outcome. You are comfortable in your own skin, and you may be consistent, but you are not rushed or desperate.

Overall, the key difference between chasing and pursuing a woman is the attitude and approach that the man takes. Chasing can be seen as desperate and unconfident while pursuing can be seen as confident and respectful. When you are chasing, you have a scarcity mindset; when you are pursuing, you are going after something you want.

<u>Example of chasing:</u>

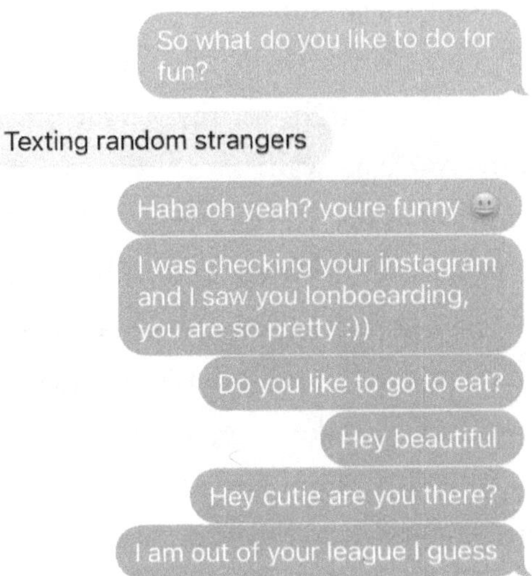

When you are jumping ahead and asking too many questions, you are showing too much interest at once, and that comes off as low value, and you make it easy for the girl not to text you back and take you seriously because you are coming off too strong.

Pursuing is different. You are present in the conversation but flow with her:

You are intentional; you show her that you are interested in her but don't come as desperate as the other example. You have a much more chill, going-with-the-flow vibe. You communicate that you respect yourself enough to see when things aren't being reciprocated, and you can walk away. He is not trying to force things or to manipulate the woman into liking him but is instead taking the time to get to know her and to build a connection with her. This approach can be seen as more attractive and desirable than chasing, as it shows that the man is confident and self-assured and that he is willing to take things slow If you are pursuing a woman. When your efforts are not reciprocated after a while, but you keep going and persisting but still get nothing back, which will get you into the chasing category. Do not cross that line. Respect yourself and know when you walk away.

We will learn how to ask her out properly by following a process in chapter 4, "Context In The Process"

Nice Guys do Finish last

No More Mr. Nice Guy

Most men were raised by their families to be a gentleman. We all heard it. Buy flowers, pay for the meals, open the door, pull out the chair, carry her bag, give her your seat, etc. We all grew up watching this type of behavior in movies, and they show that the guy who does all this, insists the most, and is the most romantic is the one who gets the girl, and they live happily ever after. If you are the type of guy, girls say things like: " You are a good friend," " You are such a nice guy," "you will find a lovely lady one day," Etc. You are probably the "Nice Guy." Do you feel like you always get walked all over? Are you the type of guy that is always there for a woman?

What do you need? What can I do for you? You are there to do whatever she needs whenever she needs it. If she texts you about another guy, you are consoling her.

There is nothing wrong with being a nice person, but if you are that type of guy that is sexually interested in a woman and you let her put you what you really want from her with the hope that one day she will consider it for sexual or relationship access. YOU NEED TO STOP RIGHT NOW. Do you only do this with the hopes that one day she will get interested in you and fuck or give you a chance because of all these things you are doing for her? I am sorry to tell you that it rarely happens.

You need to put yourself first before her. You don't have to be a dick, but if you are sexually interested in a woman, make your intentions clear with her because being her beta male friend won't work to get her to consider you sexually. You cannot allow this to happen any longer. When a man puts on a facade of niceness in order to win a woman's affection, it can be perceived as manipulative and insincere. This can make the woman feel as if the man is not genuine and instead tries to manipulate her into liking him. Additionally, the "nice guy" is often seen as being overly passive and lacking in assertiveness, which can be unattractive to many women. Instead, women often find confident and self-assured men more attractive, as these qualities suggest that the man is comfortable in his own skin and is not afraid to be himself. The problem that is seen with many guys stuck in this behavior is that they don't think they have any alternatives for what they are doing, and they keep themselves in the same people-pleasing position when it is clear that it is not working for them. Nice guys will tell you they get nothing out of being like that. Men often get this confused; they think they need to be an asshole and not necessarily.

"Nice Guy" is a term to describe the typical man that is too agreeable, vulnerable, and unassertive. He does not stand up for himself, has no boundaries, no backbone, or life, and puts other people's needs before his own. He avoids confrontations, and when it comes to women, He lets them walk all over to get some compliance. There is nothing wrong with being nice; you just lack the masculine traits women find attractive in a man. Being like this leaves you with irrational anger and with a sense of entitlement for either sexual or romantic attention from women just because you considered yourself to be "Nice." This is also called " The Nice Guy Syndrome."

The reality is that most women do not find "Nice guys" attractive, and they will almost always put you in the friend zone. Once you are there, it is tough to get out. Sometimes you can do it, but most of the time, you have already screwed your chances and have to move on.

Women are very well aware of these types of guys; they know that many of them will just simp for sex, and they find this behavior repulsive.

Here are some of the most common mistakes that "nice guys" make when trying to date or pursue relationships with women:

The Typical Generic Compliments:

Nice guys are repetitive, boring, and predictable. They do everything to please the girl but fail to make an emotional impact. They text things like:

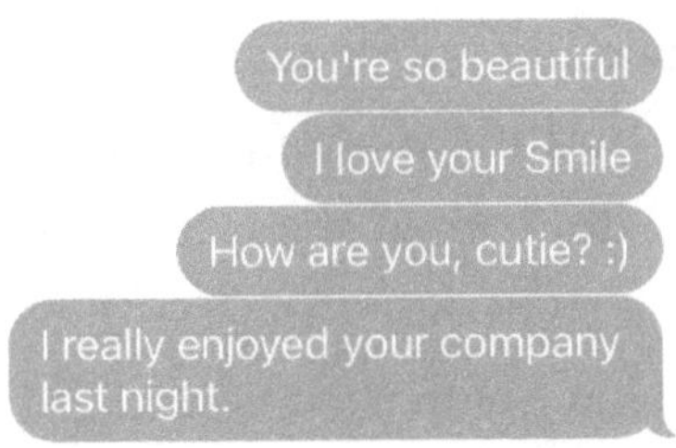

And Sometimes Long Messages like:

"Hey, I just wanted to let you know that I think you're really beautiful, and I would love to take you out sometime You seem like such a kind and interesting person, and I think we could have a lot of fun together.

Let me know if you're interested, and we can figure out a time to meet up."

"Hello, I hope you're having a great day. I just wanted to reach out and say that I think you're an amazing person and I would love the opportunity to get to know you better. I'm a really nice guy and I promise I'll treat you well. Let me know if you're interested in going out sometime and we can make it happen."

"I know this might be a little out of the blue but I just had to tell you how much I enjoy your company. You're so smart, funny, and interesting, and I would love the chance to spend more time with you"

And on top of that, they add a heart emoji. You have already fallen into the nice guy trap. You probably think that the more compliments you give her, the more attracted she will be towards you. Women get compliments like this all the time, and they are kinda tired of it. These texts are super common and generic, and it makes women think, "Just another of those dudes". So what you need to do, especially at the beginning, is keep those compliments to a minimum, and if you compliment her, make it more creative and unique and do it when she is investing in the conversation. Do not validate her right out the gate. Keep it to the occasion and timing that you have with the women.

Women should earn your validation and your attention. Don't just give it out like that. Give compliments once she starts investing. We will talk about how to compliment women correctly in chapter 4.

Agreeing with Everything She says:

Typical Nice Guy behavior. You praise everything she says and are too agreeable in your conversations with her. It doesn't mean you have to be confrontational and always argue with everything. But if you have a different opinion than hers or you don't necessarily agree with something she is saying. Don't be afraid of expressing those feelings or contradicting her sometimes. Or at least do not say yes to everything. Just don't be the "yes" man. She will sense that, and it will turn her off.

Focusing Too Much on the Woman's Needs and Not Enough on Their Own:

"Nice guys" often put women's needs and desires ahead of their own, to the point where they neglect their own happiness and well-being. This can lead to resentment, bitterness, and a lack of fulfillment in their relationships.

Backtracking if She Acts Offended:

If you were a jerk about something or you have to say sorry for a situation that you screwed up, of course. Apologize; there is nothing wrong with that. But there is a time and place for everything. You do not need to be always apologetic even when you don't have to. To give you an example: You guys are talking; let's say you make a random, inoffensive, soft joke about her zodiac sign, and now she gets offended or acts offended as a shit test. Women sometimes will shit-test you like that. The worst thing you can do is apologize and backtrack with messages like 'just kidding, lol.' or "I am sorry with a sad face :(." Nice guys will do whatever they can to diffuse tension and avoid conflict, and they will be very afraid of offending women. Many women these days get offended easily for things they should not be offended at, so get used to it. Also, If you backtrack like that, she has no reason to trust any word you say, and you will become unconfident and weak. "Nice guys" are usually unconfident, insecure, and weak. If that happens and you know she acted offended for something that you should not have to apologize for, you can do things like laugh it out, agree and exaggerate, troll her back or insert humor into the tension she may have caused. If she keeps going, call out her behavior. We will go into more de details about how to deal with shit tests or situations like this in chapter 4.

Over-Investing:

If you are texting her, and she texts you back with one-word responses, and you respond with paragraphs. Or maybe she hasn't even responded to you, and you double-texted again with another paragraph. You get very insecure and anxious when you don't get a response That comes off as needy, desperate, and low value. When texting, your investment should equal hers, do not invest more until she invests more. If she doesn't respond, give it a few days until you re-open her. Get a life, and do not be by the phone waiting for her response. Text and forget.

Asking the Typical

<u>how are you doing questions:</u>

Asking a girl how she is doing, how her day was, how is work, how her shift was, etc. I get it is polite and nice. It shows you care, right? Well, the problem is that, especially at the beginning. Doing this too much won't spike interest in the girl, and it will make her roll her eyes instead of considering you sexually, romantically or both. She is more likely to ignore you and respond to the guy who is either not texting her those typical generic texts, sends her a more creative, fun, and interesting text, and is not chasing her. If you do it sometimes totally fine, the problem is when you overdo it and lead with it going in circles with it.

Being her texting buddy:

You are keeping her entertained. That is so nice of you!

You have been going back in forth talking with her for hours talking about random stupid shit. You may think that is good because she is actually replying to you, but deep down, especially if you and she are getting to know each other, she will think you have nothing better to do than text with a random girl all day. Women want to date men with busy and active lives. You should not have a lifestyle that allows you to text her all day. You only need to talk 2-3 days a week when you first get to know each other. There is no need to be texting 24/7. All those random conversation topics you can have in person.

Text back and forth a little bit. That's fine but use the phone mainly to set up a date and get off the phone.

Being too available:

You are always there, that is very nice of you but is not helping you.

<u>Take a look at this example:</u>

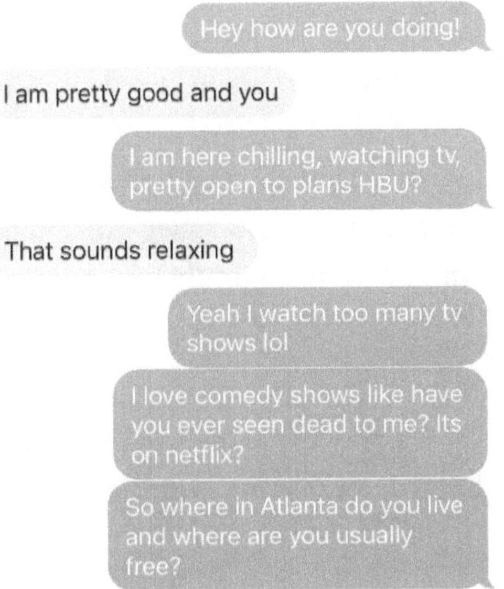

With these behaviors, you come off as "I got nothing going on!, can we hang out? Many guys are so needy that in almost every text they send the girl, they respond right away and come off as if they are always there for her. You respond to her message right away every time. You are able to meet any day at any time. Basically, you are always present. With behaviors of always acting like you are there for her, you are implying that you have nothing going on and your life and you care too much about her and seeing her. Show that you have activities and hobbies and that you are not a dude who is always doing nothing and will be available whenever she pleases.

These are the types of behaviors that make women put you in the friend zone or get you ghosted. Women like an assertive man who is not scared to go after what he wants and is firm in their direction and has their own life. At the same time, do not fall into the trap of being the asshole that you cannot have a conversation with. It is only about not letting women walk all over you and increasing your perceived value.

There is something that you need to understand about women. They are not like us. They are backward as hell, and they tend to date up. That means they will be interested in a man they perceive to be of higher value than they are. Women have tons of guys texting them and blowing up their phones, and they typically ignore most of them and chase and sleep with the few guys they perceive to be high value.

Most men don't know the game from a female perspective and have no idea how different the world is and feels from their viewpoint.

Don't get me wrong at the beginning. You have to be the one doing most of the pursuing. And listen to the word I used, "pursuing," Not "chasing." You already learned that these two are completely different. You are most likely to fall into the beta male orbiter category when you are the nice guy. You cannot always be chasing and pedestalizing a woman. Almost every woman out there is a nice guy that is basically just talking to themselves. Be a nice person, of course, do not be an obnoxious guy that treats her badly, just have a backbone, and don't be her dancing monkey.

Being too passive and
Not Standing Up for Themselves:

"Nice guys" often have difficulty setting boundaries and communicating their needs and desires. They may be afraid of being seen as "mean" or "selfish," so they go along with whatever the woman wants, even if it goes against their own wishes.

Trying too hard to please the woman and
Not Being Themselves:

"Nice guys" often try to be who they think the woman wants them to be, rather than being their authentic selves. This can lead to a lack of genuine connection and intimacy and feelings of inauthenticity and resentment.

CHAPTER 2

NAVIGATING THE WORLD OF MODERN DATING

We live in a world of social media and dating apps. Over the last 20 years, the world has been digitalizing at a fast pace. We are more connected than ever but, at the same time, more disconnected than ever. Dating in the social media age is quite different from dating in the past.

One of the biggest changes is the proliferation of online dating platforms, which have made it easier for people to meet and connect with potential partners. Technology has affected people's lives in a way that they don't even realize. Dating and the way that individuals build romantic relationships are one of them. And unfortunately, more things changed for the worse than for the better. This doesn't mean you cannot improve your current dating situation, but you need to be aware of how we are as a whole and why you, along with millions of other men, are having the exact same problem and are struggling so much with dating. You have to adapt to the new sating standards and the new rules that we have today with the current system.

<u>Understanding the New Rules of the Game:</u>

We are in a unique moment in history. Social media and dating apps have globalized and transformed dating into a marketplace. A sexual marketplace. Unfortunately, people are seen as commodities as opposed to individuals. In previous generations, things were different.

For example, in the past, people stayed in communities longer, knew people more deeply, and relationships were built into getting to know each other and falling in love. Now, this has come to how you present yourself and what you have to offer. Before having social media and dating apps, men and women used to get to know each other through their surroundings and environments. Women would mostly date guys in their social circle, such as her job, college, her group of friends, etc. This meant that women were more confined to being with men at their level, circle, and city. Nowadays, there are more people moving around, people are staying in jobs, schools, and relationships for a shorter period of time, there is less sense of community, and relationships are now based more on advertised value and presentation instead of coexistence and familiarity. This hasn't benefited men when it comes to dating. Because of social media and dating apps and the expectation of men always having to initiate, women these days have a lot of options, and men are throwing themselves at them in the daily basics.

Even women who are not that attractive get attention from men, she may be a 6, but she thinks and acts like a nine because of all the validation that she gets. What this has done is it has given women an abundance mindset and an inflated sense of ego. So the problem we are facing is that many women, even though they may not be that attractive, still receive constant attention and validation from men, which makes their egos go through the roof, and male attention doesn't have the value that it once had. Chasing, constant compliments, and simping are very common to them. High-value men do not do this, nice guys and thirsty beta males do, but since there are more out there behaving the wrong way, they are making things harder for the rest of us. According to a study published by Wapoand and substantiated by the GSS data, Male virginity is on the rise. Men are losing their virginity much later and having fewer sexual partners than previous generations, and this started spiking in 2008 when Social Media was becoming more prevalent. So women have more options than ever before. They are getting bombarded with texts by all these guys trying to get with them all the time. But do not get discouraged. See it in a way that things have become different more than harder. So as you see, It is not entirely your fault. But it is partially your fault, which is good because there are things in your control that you can do to improve your situation. Do not dare to give up. Many men are giving up on dating, which is good news for you because there is less competition to deal with. And if you bought this book because you don't intend to give up, that's great news. Things are different now but keep this in mind, by past standards, it was easier to achieve average success but harder to achieve extraordinary success. Now it is harder to achieve average success but easier to achieve extraordinary success than it was before. See this as an opportunity rather than a discouragement.

If you take steps to improve your dating life and start that by texting more effectively, you can scale this, and the number of women you are dating will increase. Use these skills to achieve whatever you want, either to build a rotation of women you are constantly seeing and hooking up with or to get your dream girlfriend and the relationship you want.

Do not rehash or wish things could be different. Dwelling on it is not going to change your reality. Accept it for what it is and act upon it. There is good news when it comes to this if you are the type of guy who is self-aware and you start working on your social skills, your texting game which this book will teach you. Improve yourself, and you will open the doors to many opportunities.

<u>Men Are Struggling With Modern dating:</u>

Unfortunately, these days most men struggle with women and relationships. As we mentioned early in the book, male virginity is rising. In 2021, 1 out of 3 men reported no sexual activity over the past year; men also lost their virginity much later and had fewer sexual partners than in previous generations. Most guys don't deal with women too often and are trapped in an echo chamber of social media, dating apps, video games, and porn. This is one of the reasons modern men have lower testosterone than their fathers and grandfathers had when they were their age. Women deal way more with the opposite sex, far more than we do. A lot of men have social anxiety and no drive to do anything. They are constantly staring at a screen to receive a rush of dopamine. The nature and backbone that men should naturally develop to talk to women and get ahead in life are getting lost by the day.

There are a few reasons for this. But mainly with the rise of social media and dating apps, women now have many options and access to men they didn't have before. Since women tend to date up, meaning they tend to date a guy they perceive has a higher status than they do, a greater number of women are being attracted to a smaller number of men, and on the flip side, a greater number of men have problems attracting women. With this dating scene, opportunities for average heterosexual men diminish since women's standards go up. This is one reason why over half of dating app users are men. This has left most men out of the dating pool, and it is only expected to worsen. For men who don't take action to improve their situation, they are going to have a rough time with women. Younger and middle-aged men are the loneliest that have ever been in generations. The incel movement is growing every year, and it seems like all women are chasing the top 10-20 percent of men out there. Men in this situation of being out of the game get themselves into a vicious cycle where if they don't make moves to get themselves out of that situation, it will get worse and worse for them. But if you start making moves day after day, week after week, year after year to change your situation, reading this book now, for example. You will be in a different position a few years from now. So there is hope, and it all depends on you. . Now you know why you are here, this book will teach you to text women in a way that benefits you.

Patience pays With Women

You will learn that we as men need to do better at being more patient when it comes to women and dating. As a man, I understand where we are coming from. We want so much to happen soo soon. We want to see her as quickly as possible and hook up as soon as possible. We want instant gratification, and it makes us move faster than we should a lot of the time. Male sexual drive plays the main role in this, which is different from female sex drive. We get turned on by our eyes, so we are constantly turned on by seeing. Women's sex drive, on the other hand, doesn't work that way. Your looks get your foot in the door, but other things need to be in place for her to be turned on. This causes us to skip steps in the process, and skipping steps with women rarely works. This is so common that every woman has run into an impatient, needy man in her life that rushes things with her. This is why one of the ways women test men is by making them wait for dates or sex to see how calibrated he is and how different from all the other men she has been with. Women find patience in men attractive, and they see you as a socially calibrated, put-together man. They may not say this, but deep in them, they want to work for your attention.

You are fighting with your instincts here, so you must first be aware of this and why it happens. That natural thirst, you need to learn to control it, and the easiest way for you to do that is by being on your purpose and working on your goals. Whatever your mission is in life, whatever you are trying to accomplish, whatever lifestyle you want to have, that should be your priority and your main focus. Put yourself first and pursue whatever you want out of women on the side.

Being focused on your purpose cuts that thirst, I would say, at least in half. Ask yourself: What are you doing with your days? Are you working? What are you doing after work? Do you have a business, a career, dreams, hobbies, or goals? Do you have a social circle that is fulfilling? What type of lifestyle do you want to have five years from now? What about ten years from now? Are you healthy? Are you in shape? Do you work out? Are you emotionally and socially intelligent to pursue women? are you working to better yourself every day?

These things designed to help you live the life you want are what matters and where your focus should be. When you have this mindset, you are not impatient and rushing things with women. Of course, you want to move as fast as possible, but you are comfortable. You flow with the process naturally and smoothly since you also do not have the time to worry so much about it. The more patience, layback, and less available you seem to her. The more you will motivate her to move faster with you. You want to keep it simple: Hang out, have fun and hook up.

Please do not get me wrong; with this, I am not saying you have to be lazy and take no action. I am not saying you don't have to make moves to get the date as soon as possible, and you have to wait months for the meetup or to have sex with her. You should move at the fastest pace you can, just do not rush it with her. It can sometimes happen that it takes a while for both of your schedules to line up, go to the correct pace depending of your situation and hers. Also, when you are texting and talking to different women is a lot easier on your patience than when you are only talking to one woman. If you worry a lot about this woman you're texting, your day is based on her; you're thinking all the time about her that's the problem right there. Once you start seeing results, it will be easier for you to be like this on default.

Your competence will become your confidence. When you are in flow with your life, you will realize that you just have to do you, work on your stuff, be patient, take things slow, and you will be fine.

So don't back off and get lazy. I have to give these disclaimers to ensure guys don't take it wrong. If you find yourself impatient about many of the tips here of waiting and not overthinking about a girl not responding to your text is maybe because you don't have a life. You need to focus on yourself and keep the pursuit natural at your own pace; this is not hard to do when you are busy with your life but tough to do if you have nothing going on for yourself. Having a life and a purpose in life is attractive to women.

The Importance Of Being On Your purpose:

Busy men who are ambitious, goal-driven, and focused on their purpose don't have a problem and flow naturally with the game of texting and life, for that matter. When you have a busy schedule, and you are working on getting to where you want to be is extremely attractive to women; they get into a competition mode with that, and also that thirst and neediness that youhave for that woman leaves and it makes it easier for you not to be desperate.

Finding your purpose is not easy for people; it all comes to you, what you want out of life, the lifestyle you want to live. We all want different things in life. If you are a guy who is lost in life, you are not very satisfied with your life in general, you're broke, you are not in the best shape, and you don't know what you want, we have all been there at some point, that's ok, my advice to you is to take some time away from dating and focus on yourself. Focus on improving yourself to improve your situation. Look at your life right now, your job, and your career, and think about the lifestyle you want to live. What would be your version of success?

Some people want to get married and have kids and a successful job; other people want to chase a specific career; you may be money motivated, and you want to be making a particular amount of money, or maybe you want only to be financially independent to live life on your own terms and do whatever you want to do. You must find your ideal lifestyle; working towards that is your purpose, and it should always come first. Keep the main thing, the main thing.

So when you are in a position where you are constantly working on getting where you want to be, you don't have the time to get needy about women or worry about why she doesn't reply to you, let alone chase a woman. Chasing a woman is just degrading to you when you have this mindset. When you are working every day to make your future the best it can possibly be, you have an abundance mindset, and you approach dating differently. Your sense of purpose and success guides you every day throughout the years.

If you can portray this to the woman you are dating, she will be extremely attractive to you. Women notice these things, and they go towards men like this. Women are not chasing the men chasing them; They are chasing the men that are chasing their purpose in life.

Having this mindset gives you a sense of a meaningful life, which contributes to better mental and physical health and, in the case of women, being more successful with them as well. If you do not find it right away, that is completely fine, it is a lifestyle journey, and you will probably find it throughout the years. Having a sense of purpose and direction in life can bring a sense of fulfillment and satisfaction. It can give you a sense of meaning and direction and help you feel more motivated and engaged in your daily activities. Finding your purpose may take years or a lifetime; that is something for you to figure out and evaluate what is that you want out of. One way is to ask yourself what type of lifestyle you want to live 5-10 years from now.

Where do you see yourself in the future?
Where do you want to be living?
What do you want to be doing?

Being on your purpose means having a clear sense of what you want to accomplish in life and why it is important to you. It is about knowing what you are passionate about and what drives you, and using this knowledge to guide your decisions and actions. For some people, their purpose may be related to their career or profession, such as pursuing a specific job or achieving a certain level of success in their field. For others, their purpose may be more personal or spiritual, such as pursuing personal growth or positively impacting the world. No matter your purpose, it should be meaningful and important to you, which motivates you to strive for success, and fulfillment, and your main thing will be chasing that objective. Whatever it is in life that will bring you ultimate joy. This is an essential part of living a fulfilling and healthy life, and it can help you feel more satisfied, motivated, and engaged and improve your mental and physical well-being.

CHAPTER 3

THE 14TH MOST COMMON MISTAKES MEN MAKE WHEN TEXTING WOMEN

In this chapter, we will explore the 14 most common mistakes that men make when texting women.

Mistake#1:

<u>Texting all the time. Long paragraphs. All about you:</u>

Many guys do this. They only talk about themselves with women and try to fit everything they do into one paragraph when texting them. This is a huge mistake. Especially at the beginning when you are getting to know each other. If you need to text long paragraphs texts is because you need to express a big idea or tell a story about a situation. When you are in the beginning stages of a conversation, there is no need to send long texts. Keep it short and to the point. And forget about you; keep it about her. That is how you get her to invest; this makes you more attractive in her eyes. Sometimes if the situation calls for it, you can send a long text about yourself. But if you really need to express an idea and it is too long of a text, maybe you want to send a voice message or call her.

<u>Take a look at this example:</u>

Too long and not necessary to expand so much. Many men do this, and I am sure you have done it before. There is no need to be overly wordy and tell her so much about you when texting. A better response to that would have been something like

Keep it simple, don't be overly wordy. Comes off as low value.

Mistake #2:

<u>Putting the girl on a pedestal</u>

Pedestalizing women doesn't benefit you or her in any way. Attractive women are not saints; they are not perfect; she is a flawed human just like you. There is no reason to convince yourself or act like she is perfect; there is nothing wrong with her. When men pedestalize, women is usually not reciprocated, and it is mostly one-sided. Meaning you are pedestalizing her, but she is not doing anything back to you. Behaving like this doesnt get the woman to like you; on the contrary, it kills the attraction and makes her look down on you. If you treat her like a celebrity, she will treat you like a fan. She will make you an option instead of a priority.

Pedestalizing is basically SIMPING, which is one of the reasons why many of these women have such big egos and don't respect men and treat them like dogs. Now you may be doing this without realizing it. Awareness in it of itself is transformative, so now you know you need to stop.

Doing this comes off as low value, and it doesnt show you have an abundance mindset. It is ok to compliment her here and there and be a gentleman. If you are in a relationship with her, you want to treat her well. But there is no reason to always treat her like the queen of England.

Mistake# 3:

<u>You are too boring:</u>

You either go to one extreme or the other. I know I said you have to make it simpler and text less, but it doesn't mean you have to be bold and boring. You show no emotion, no excitement. Talking to you is like talking to a wall. Don't do this. Just because you need to text less doesn't mean you need to be boring. You need to be interesting, funny, and you need to portray yourself as a high-value man so that you can have an interesting and valuable conversation.

Take a look at this example:

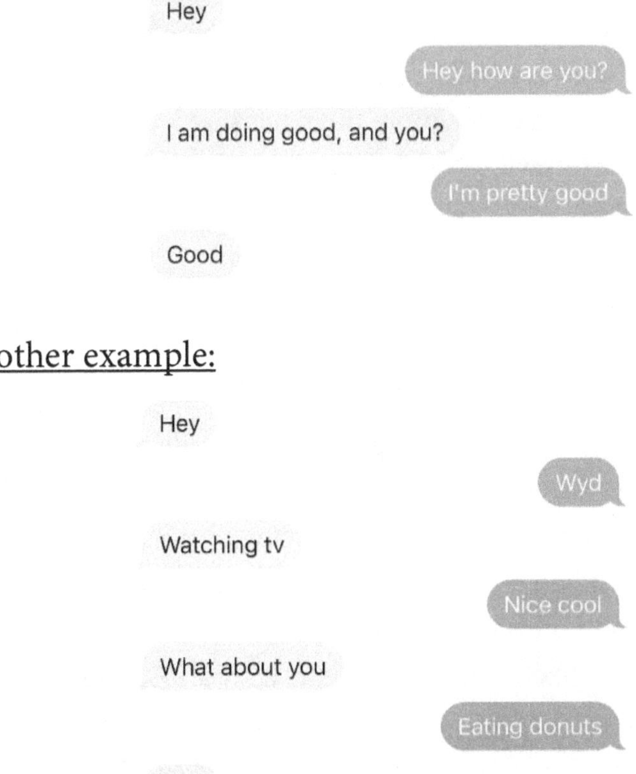

Another example:

Is texting this way going to cause anyone to want to reply and talk to you long-term? The answer is no. Have common sense. Just because you realize that you are texting too much and need to do less doesnt mean you are doing nothing. No girl or guy wants to talk to a wall.

Mistake # 4:

Using long openers/ Pickup lines

Many men think that when they are first talking to a woman, either on a dating app or sending the first text, they must send creative long pickup lines and long openers three sentences long to impress her. You don't; you want to keep your openers simple and casual. Keeping it simple and to the point is the best way to get responses. If you met in person, the first texts could be something brief; you definitely don't need to text a pickup line. Girls are so used to guys doing this, and they mostly ignore them because it comes off as low value and you are trying too hard. The best is to keep openers simple. We will expand on this later in the book.

Mistake # 5:

You are always the one initiating

Don't get me wrong, at the beginning, you will need to initiate more than her. She will not initiate a conversation until she is invested at least a little bit. But even if she is invested in you, she will not initiate if you are not giving her space to miss you and text you. If you are always the one texting her first, she will take you for granted. Women like to be with a man with a life, and his world doesn't revolve around her. And honestly, you should not have the time to text her all the time. Once you have seen each other and she is invested in the conversation, give her and yourself some space. You may not need to talk to her if you know that you won't be able to set up a date that week. If you do this, you will see that little by little; she will initiate and open a conversation with you. This takes time, but nothing happens overnight.

Mistake # 6:

<u>Using too many emojis</u>

Using a few emojis here and there is acceptable and not a big deal. But if you see yourself using emojis in almost every message you send, and you end up using more emojis than her. That's where the problem is, and you need to stop that immediately, especially those heart emojis validating her. That is not masculine, and it comes off as immature and feminine. Your texts must imply masculinity and maturity. Keep emojis to a minimum, mainly to display a feeling here and there. Avoid heart emojis. Leave that to the girl to use.

Mistake # 7:

<u>Not closing the optimal way.</u>

It is extremely common and the main reason you cannot get it when you ask for the meetup many times. What a lot of men do is they are talking to a girl and randomly ask her out of thenblue, or in a way, she will most likely say no or not reply at all. There is a process to asking a girl out in a way she is more likely to accept and comply, and if you are in sales, you know what I am talking about, but most guys tend to skip steps and just ask the girl out randomly sometimes when they are not even talking about meeting up. Don't do that. Follow a process of building investment first, then get the girl to agree to the general idea of meeting up with you; then, you have to figure out her schedule and proceed to a soft close and then a hard close. We will cover this more in-depth in chapter 4.

Mistake#8:

<u>Texting her back right away every time.</u>

This is a very typical mistake for beginners. EVERY SINGLE time she texts you, 2 minutes later, you send your reply. Guys that don't have much of a life, don't get that much attention from women, and don't have much experience are guilty of this. So when they do get a girl to text them back, they get excited, and as soon as she texts them, they reply right back. If you are texting a girl and you respond to her every single time within minutes of her texts, I can assure you the conversation will not get much further. Inside her head, she will think you have nothing better to do than message her all day. And this is worse if you text her immediately every time you combine it with long texts. There is a time and place to text back soon, like if you are having an actively engaging conversation about a topic or sexting. But most of the time, you want to wait a few hours before responding or be legitimately busy and respond to her when you have time. If she always takes hours to respond, do not reward that.

Mistake#9:

<u>Being Awkward and Saying Weird Shit</u>

Almost every woman out there experienced more than once guys that are just weird and awfully awkward when texting. They bring up random conversation topics out of the blue. They start talking about random situations, or they just say weird shit that has nothing to do with the prior conversation or her.

<u>Take a look at this example:</u>

Did that make a lot of sense to you? How did that text make you feel? The creativity that so many guys have to make it as weird as possible is amazing. I don't know what happens in a lot of men's heads sometimes, but almost every girl out there can tell you that they have just so many men writing weird shit like that that is random and out of context. Comes off as weird and cringe. This comes from a mix of being impulsive, not being very socially calibrated, and with a lack of understanding about text game and not knowing there is a process to getting a girl to go out with you or have sex with you. They just say whatever comes to mind, even if it doesn't make that much sense, because you don't think before you act.

You may think this is not you, and you would never do something stupid like that or you may have done it before. But you would be surprised by the number of guys that text weird shit all the time to women. This is why you need to be self-aware of what you are doing, the situation with the women you are texting, and where you are in the process, and not just pull things out of your butt randomly.

Mistake #10:

<u>Getting Butthurt</u>

This is a very common problem for women, they are very aware of this, and this is something that they constantly have to watch out for. "Nice Guys" are guilty of this. Often guys show interest, sometimes way too much interest; they send shitty pickup lines and openers and just come off too strong and clingy to the girl. Then when the girl rejects them or just doesn't show compliance, they get triggered and start insulting the girl or attacking them. This is something most women have gone thru in their lives. That's one of the reasons why a girl won't respond to you or just won't be upfront to reject you in real life because she doesn't want you to get butthurt and make a scene.

<u>Take a look at this example.</u>

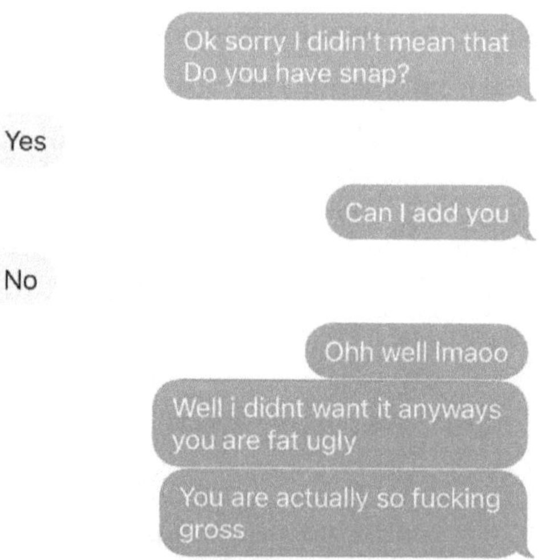

Not only your text game sucks, but when you don't get the response you were expecting because of your bad texting game, you get butthurt. The solution is to improve your text game to increase the chances of her complying, and when a woman does reject you in a text or in person, the right way to handle that is just to laugh it off and try to get compliance a bit later. Once you get butthurt and you make a scene. It's over. High-value men don't act this way, but nice guys do. So make the switch. Be patient, laugh it out, and don't have a bad texting game in the first place so you can decrease your chances of being rejected in the first place. But if she does: Tease her a bit, play with her and try better again next time.

Mistake #11:

<u>Constant and Consistent spelling errors.</u>

All of us have spelling errors. I am not trying to tell you that you must be perfect when texting. A little bit is completely fine, and the women probably will not even notice it. But if you constantly have bad grammar when texting, you make consistent spelling mistakes for simple things you should know how to write, which is not salvageable. You can avoid this by double-checking every text you write before sending it, especially if you tend to make many grammatical mistakes. If English is not your first language is totally fine. You will make more errors than the rest of us. A good tip is to let the woman know that English is not your first language and say that you're sorry if you make a mistake here in there. That way, it won't matter that much. Just keep them in check and don't let it be too excessive, that's all.

Mistake #12:

<u>Calling the girl out of the blue</u>

You are texting a girl; you think everything is going well. And suddenly, for whatever reason, you dial her number and call her randomly without even letting her know, or even worse: Facetiming her. Why did you do that? she was not expecting that. Most of us do not like to be called randomly, not only women. If you are in a relationship, this is completely ok to do, but in the beginning, it is not. You would be surprised how many guys do this. Girls also don't like to talk on the phone that much if they don't know you because they get awkward and nervous. If you want to talk to her on the phone, ask yourself why you want to talk to her, what are you are trying to do, and what do expect to get out of the call. And If you decide that you still want to call her, set up the phone over text first. Let her know you want to call her or ask if she would like to talk on the phone with you first. Have her expect your phone call.

Mistake#13:

<u>Not sexualizing the right way</u>

Sexting. I would say that over 90 percent of guys do not know how to sexualize the right way and turn women on. They end up turning her off. Only a few of you are doing it the right way. They are texting the girl, she shows a little bit of attraction or compliance, and randomly you send her a sexual text. Good sexting is supposed to be very smooth and progressive. The girl should never feel like: "Ohh, where does this come from?" Test the waters first and then move things forward slowly. Unfortunately, guys like to skip steps and jump out, and one text is significantly different from the other text.

Women need the build-up and that sexual tension. Good sexting should be progressive and not random. Chapter 6 will go into the details of sexting the right way.

Mistake #14:

<u>You're too available</u>

Nice guys make this mistake a lot. You're always available right away. 24/7 You are just there for her. You respond to her right way no matter what time of the day it is; you meet with her whenever she wants or can. You are just basically there for her. If you do this to women that you are starting to date, what you are communicating is that you have nothing going on with your life, that you are probably not very successful, that she is your only option and that you have nothing better to do than text her all the time. You are not a challenge. You will always be there for her, and you are her back-end call. You are setting yourself up for failure with women. Why would she want to see you if you text her all day? You will do most of the attraction and the selling of yourself in person. The phone is not to be texting back and forth all day. You will mainly use it for keeping attraction and setting appointments. Have a life, be working on your goals, and don't prioritize texting her all the time. Show her you are a busy man and that you have a life by cutting this behavior and not being so available all the time.

CHAPTER 4

CONTEXT IN THE PROCESS

In this chapter, we will go from the basics to more advanced techniques and tips to text women effectively from start to finish. Everything goes from the opening, how you introduce yourself, your conversational style, and building investment. The purpose at first is to raise the level of interest she has in you. Once you build some interest, you go for the date. You want to see her and hook up, correct? That is the purpose of texting her. It is a tool for you to get to meet the girl. You can talk a little bit and build attraction enough to go for the meetup, but important, long, deep conversations should be left when you are with her in person. The problem is that many we think that since there are a lot of guys texting her and being in her face, we need to be in her face more than these other guys, in other words, be another beta male orbiter because if we don't do that, she is going to be distracted by these other guys. You do not need to constantly communicate with her for her to like you. . Once you have built a bit of investment, it is time to go for the meetup; if you wait too long, a girl's subconscious mind thinks you are not a bold guy that goes after what he wants, and many times, they get bored, if you go too soon you may not get compliance. It has to be a bit later once the conversation starts to flow when she knows a little bit about you but not too much when you are still somewhat of a stranger but not a complete stranger. Typically around the 10th-15th text.

Starting a

<u>Conversation:</u>

Depending on how you start the conversation with a woman, the harder or easier it will be for you to get your desired outcome. it is essential that you begin talking to a woman to get anywhere. Texting a girl to make plans for later is the new status quote of dating. There are a lot of different situations where you can meet a girl, and knowing how to start a conversation will depend on your specific situation with that particular person.

- You will meet women at school or work
- You will meet women on dating apps
- You will meet women at night if you like to go out
- You will meet women from cold approach if you have the balls to do it.
- You will meet women at social events or gatherings you go to.

Of course, there are countless other ways you can meet women, and I cannot say every single one, but those are the main ways. There is a significant difference between texting a girl you are already in a relationship with and texting a girl you have just met or recently dating. Before we get into the details of how to text depending on different situations and I want to give you an overview of how things should naturally work for a successful relationship or dating which favors you as a man.

When you first start texting a girl, there is no secret that at the beginning, you will be doing most of the pursuing, not chasing, pursuing. Expect that, which is the way that works most of the time and for most of history. Now she will have a perceived value of yourself. You are a high-value man who has a life and is focused on his purpose, and you are interested in her. That is what should be the case and how she should perceive it. Perception is reality, and if she does not perceive you as a high-value man, she will not be that interested in you. It all depends on your behavior. So you have her number, and the goal is for you both to hang out. You will text for a little bit if you want to create a bit of attraction and investment. Once you get to this point, you want to ask her out and get her to go on a first date with you. Assuming that on the date, everything went well. , there was chemistry and attraction between both of you, and if you did everything right, you should go for the first kiss if it]]this doesn't happen in the first date, fine, no big deal as soon as you can get it to meet you with you a second time you can give it a try there.

You want to try to hook up with her by the second or third date; this way so you can get the sex out of the way quickly, and you can actually enjoy the girl's company without you trying to do something. If the first date goes well, you start your routine again and mostly leave her alone until your next meeting. Conversations should be nothing crazy, and her investment will depend on the women's attraction level towards you. But you want to keep it casual and quick if she is interested and you don't make any significant mistakes, she will go out with you again. Most girls will sleep with you by the second or third date. The more she likes you, the more she will open up her schedule for you. Assuming her level of attraction is high for you, you have been doing most things right, and she likes you. Once you get to the point with a woman when you start seeing each other once a week or more and you have been hooking up often, she should start investing more in the conversation. Once you reach a certain point, you can back off, and she should be doing most of the texting, chasing, and pursuing. When the relationship starts developing this way and continues into the second and third months, maybe you are seeing each other 2-3 times per week. She should be the one reaching out to you more often. So in the beginning, you will invest more, but once the relationships start developing, your level of investment needs to come down, and hers should be going up. A relationship works better when a woman is chasing your validation and not the other way around. A relationship where the man is always chasing the woman and seeking her validation never works. As she reaches out more, you see her more. You never, ever bring up the relationship topic. You will only hang out, have fun and hook up. Let her bring up the "What are we" talk, and then you decide if you want to go into a deeper relationship with her or if you want her to hook up only. I know I went a little fast and did not go deep into the details. I wanted to give you a quick overview, and I wanted you to know that you will not always have to do most of the work. Most of the work will be at the beginning.

In reality, women enjoy sex the same if not more than you. They want to fuck. But a lot of guys open their mouths and talk too much. They say stupid shit and things that ultimately turn the women off. Most of the time is, we men dig our own graves.

Openers:

A lot of guys overcomplicate openers. Starting a conversation with a girl shouldn't be that hard. Most of us put a lot of pressure on ourselves to make a good impression; sometimes, we overthink and overdo it. The right thing to say will depend on your context with that girl, whether you are messaging her for the first time after you got her number in person or on a dating app. But the basis will remain the same; you want to keep it short and simple. it is the best way to start a conversation. Sending the first text when you got her number in person is simpler than opening on a dating app. When it comes to dating apps, what a lot of guys do is that they either go to one extreme or the other. They text the typical, generic, boring texts like,

Hey
Hi
Hey cutie
Hello
Hey beautiful
Hey baby
Hello gorgeous
Hey how are you
Hi sweetie how are you
Happy Monday!

You need to see this from the girl's perspective. She is getting hundreds of messages from different guys, and if you ask any girl, the majority of messages are like that. Think about it; she cannot respond to everyone and try to talk to every guy from the same opener. It would be a full-time job for her to respond to every single message. If you ask any girl to show you her dating apps or social media, it is flooded with these generic texts, but there are other types of guys that go to the other side of the spectrum, which is probably even worse. They text long openers, typically with pickup lines, random comments, or stories, complementing or validating her appearance. Please get into your head. You cannot validate a girl for free. You don't want to do any of that.

The best way to open a conversation with a girl over text will depend on a variety of factors, including your relationship with the girl, your shared interests and experiences, and the context in which you are texting her; it is when you have to use your creativity and her profile. You want to be different; among other things, you can point out unique observations about her pictures, a shared interest, ask open-ended questions or a silly joke. Something that is relevant to her and would bait her into responding.

This is awkward, I actually swiped for your dog
Ok, I'll be your boyfriend under one condition
Ohh I guess we're dating now
You look suspiciously innocent

Mention a shared interest or experience: To start the conversation, mention something you have in common with the girl, such as a shared interest or experience. This could be something that you both enjoy, such as a hobby or activity, or something that you both have experienced, such as a recent event or news story. These are just examples; you have to use your creativity on what you see on her profile, description, and pictures to come up with what to say. You want to say things to make her curious, easy to respond and catches her attention. It is important not to send something boring or cringe. Since she gets a lot of messages from different guys, you want to write something that she doesn't have to put a lot of thought into. Maybe she has a dog, maybe she has a picture travelling, and you have been there. Keep her about her and try to say something to get her to talk about herself.

You can say catching things that she either has to address it confirm it or deny it. Or open statements that she wants to know more about what you mean.

You're not crazy right?
Your pics say quite a lot about you
You seem like someone worth getting to know
Want to hear a secret?

Use her name as well. People's sweetest sound is their own name. Sometimes put her name with an exclamation point. Simple as that. Or when you are using any of the other openers, you can add her name as well.

On dating apps, things can be tough and daunting; since it is a numbers game, you have to send many different messages, and sometimes you may not text something wrong, but you won't get a response. You have to message a lot of women to get one response from a text.

Openers from a number in person:

This will be a lot simpler. It is important to remain in context, so when you are texting a girl you just met in person, sometimes the best thing to text is your intro with your name. An example of this would be like You met a girl at a bar, you can say something like:

- Hey this is andrew from the bar
- Andrew from the bar 😊

Overall, the best way to open a conversation with a girl over text is to be friendly, engaging, and genuine. By using a greeting, mentioning a shared interest or experience, and asking a question, you can start a conversation with a girl over text in a natural and engaging way. Keep it simple. Openers are meant to start a conversation, and there is no reason to overcomplicate its role.

Building her

<u>Investment and interest over time:</u>

At the beginning of the interaction, you want to be equally invested or less invested than she is. Success with texting comes from three concepts: Time, patience, and persistence. We as humans seek instant gratification with most things in life. But good things don't happen overnight. As explained before, things need to develop naturally and progressively with women. Men are rushed when it comes to their crush. We want things to develop fast. We want to be inside of her the fastest way possible but skip steps and rush things along the way. She will invest little in the beginning, so you have to be an interesting guy in her eyes. Be flirty and engaging every time that you text her. When you start getting the conversation going, mirror her response time. If she takes 5 hours to respond, do not respond minutes later.

To build investment with women over text, you will need to create a positive and engaging conversation that encourages her to continue talking to you and invest more of her time and attention in the conversation.

Some tips for building investment with women over text include:

- Ask open-ended questions: To encourage her to invest more in the conversation, ask open-ended questions that require her to provide more than just a simple yes or no answer. This will give her more opportunities to share her thoughts, feelings, and experiences and to engage more fully with the conversation.

- Show interest in her: To build investment, you must show that you are genuinely interested in her and what she has to say. This could involve asking follow-up questions, making thoughtful comments, and expressing curiosity and empathy. By showing that you are interested in her, you can encourage her to invest more in the conversation and to open up more to you.

- Be engaging and entertaining: To keep her invested in the conversation, it must be exciting to talk to you. This could involve telling interesting stories, sharing funny or relatable memes or videos, or using humor to lighten the mood. By being engaging and entertaining, you can keep her interested and invested in the conversation and encourage her to continue talking to you.

Overall, building investment with women over text requires a combination of open-ended questions, genuine interest, and engaging and entertaining conversation. By focusing on these elements, you can create a positive and engaging conversation that encourages her to invest more of her time and attention in talking to you. From an introduction to simple chatting to asking to, the meeting chat should develop between the first 10-20 texts.

As you see in that example, he is not over-investing but, at the same time, keeping it flirty and engaging. Encourage her to talk about herself. Do not make everything about you. Humans love to talk about themselves, and women are no different. But do not ask the typical boring questions most guys ask, such as "What do you do for work" "What do you like to do for fun" "How are you" Etc. This is very generic and boring. Women always get these questions from different dudes, and they are tired of it. It puts the conversation into an interview mode. First, avoid asking a whole bunch of questions. Ask fewer questions but when you ask, be creative and ask things like

What type of guys do you usually go for?
Are you close with your family?
What's your dream job?
Where did you grow up?
What are you most attracted to in a guy?

If you want to ask more flirty questions, you can ask things like

Have you ever had a one-night stand?
Has anyone ever called you a good kisser?

Of course, you would ask things like this once you get into a point of attraction and rapport with her.

You have to bait her into

<u>Investing more:</u>

Her perceiving you as a high-value man and talking about her is a good place to start. Her investment will go up and down depending on the circumstances and your behavior. You cannot control external circumstances in her life, but you can control what you do. Keep your interaction warm with her until you are able to get a meetup effectively until both of your schedules can line up.

Another way to build investment progressively and over time is by keeping the conversation relevant and about her.

People, in general, want to talk about themselves. Women are no different. Depending on your situation with that particular girl, things will be different on the surface, but the principles will be the same. If you talk about things that are relevant to her, you are most likely to get a response.

How to deal with

<u>One-Word Answers and Low-Investment Texts:</u>

This is something that every guy deals with. We all have been there and expect this to happen at the beginning of most conversations or when something happens and she goes cold. She is giving you one-word or one-sentence responses. Keep this in mind. If she responds with one-word answers and low-investment texts means her level of interest is very low. Expect this in the interaction's first stages; do not be confused about what your next move should be. You already know that you have to raise her level of interest.

This will happen a lot in a conversation where a girl is giving you one-word responses. Many times they are somehow interested in you, but they do it on purpose to see your response. If you reply short, to the point, and you keep it relevant to her, she will be more likely to keep responding, and for the conversation to keep developing, do not over-invest and reply to to long paragraphs to low-investment texts.

Many times she will not make it easy for you, and she will not give you much to work with. This will happen more when you start the conversation off social media, dating apps, a non-very successful cold approach, or in-person interactions. Whatever the situation, if she is giving you one-word answers, your first job is to know in what context. If it is a girl you just met, it is common that she will not invest a lot, and you have to get her to invest. But if a girl that you know was investing a bit but suddenly stops, you have to analyze the reason and act upon it.

First, you will not get her to invest more by you over-investing and chasing her. The person who is less interested in the conversation and willing to walk away is the person who has control of the interaction. You have to get out of that sequence first. You need to keep your perceived value as high as possible and keep the conversation relevant to her. So it will come down to value and relevance. If she perceives you as high value and you talk about something she is passionate about, her investment will be very high. If she doesnt perceives you as a high-value man, and at the same time, you talk about things she doesn't care about, her investment will be very low or non-existent. Your perceived value will come up and down depending on your behavior as she learns about you.

It can happen both ways. Maybe at the beginning, she was investing a lot because she was attracted to you, and then after learning about you, and maybe you behaved in a needy low-value way, her investment went low. On the opposite side, maybe she started investing very little, but then you acted in an interesting way, and she learned cool things about you, and she started investing more. It is definitely easier to get that interest down than up. , you need to be confident and assertive. This could involve using a strong and confident tone in your messages, or making statements or expressing opinions that show that you are confident in yourself and your abilities. By being confident and assertive, you can show the girl that you are a worthy and interesting person, and encourage her to invest more in the conversation.

Overall, if you want to raise a girl's interest in you, you need to be interesting, engaging, and confident. By focusing on these qualities, you can capture her attention and encourage her to invest more in the conversation.

Keep the conversation

Relevant to Her:

Do not talk only about your interests. At least at the beginning, where you both are getting to know each other, keep the conversation about her; talk about stuff that she is interested in, and that is relevant to her current state or stuff that involves both of you.

What is relevant is not universal. It all depends on the audience. Talking about her will get her to ask about you, and that is the best situation to talk about yourself when she ask for it and when she does, show her that you are living a cool, attractive lifestyle. Mention interesting things that you are doing. Do not tell her that you are just chilling and watching tv.

A lot of men do this; when a woman is asking what they are doing they are always chilling; this shows that you have no life at all. Every single time that you have the opportunity to say what you are doing or what you do for a living make your lifestyle sound cool and interesting.

If you see from that example, she is not investing much in the conversation, but he is not over-investing either. Matching her energy and keeping her interested at the same time. Match her texting energy while at the same time keeping it interesting and upbeat. The worst thing you can do when she is not investing too much starts over-investing and double or triple texting her. It is like chasing a cat. It will run away from you. If you message her too often, it will make you seem overeager. Not all low-investment conversations will come from being at the beginning of the interaction or from women that are interested in meeting up with you and that they will end up investing eventually.

Sometimes you will run into situations where you have to move on. If you are using dating apps, this will be common; unfortunately, a lot of girls will just waste your time because they are on dating apps only for attention and validation, and they have no intention of meeting anyone, no matter how good your text game is. If she never invests in the conversation at all from the beginning to the end of the interaction, or maybe she does invest a little bit, but at the time of meeting up, she always flakes or never wants to meet up with you. That is a sign that she is probably not interested, and you have to move on.

You already know the difference between chasing and pursuing. Once you see yourself getting into that category, she will just not invest. She will waste your time. Just move on.

Platforms:

So you are going to be texting girls on different platforms. Each platform is a little bit different. Among the most common platforms, you have Facebook, Instagram, and Snapchat. You also have dating apps like Tinder, Bumble, and Hinge, among the most popular. If you are having a conversation on any of those platforms, it is okay to keep it there for a little bit at the beginning, but as fast as possible, you want to move out of the platform into text. Many people around the world use WhatsApp as well. Having her phone number for a conversation makes it more personal than communicating thru social media or dating apps. After 7-15 texts, you should be good already to ask her number to move away from that platform. Be careful of doing this too soon.

A good way of doing this is to follow the same process and get the girl to invest in the conversation a bit and agree to the general idea of meeting with you. Once you get to the point then, you can request her phone number since it just makes sense for logistic purposes. Just simply ask what her number is in a very casual way.

Okay, sounds good, what's your #

Sounds like a plan what's your phone number?

All right, what's your number? I'll shoot you a text.

Very simple and casual. You don't need more examples. Sometimes you won't set up the date fast enough on any of these platforms because it is unreliable to depend on them to get a reply back. Also, you are competing with maybe dozens of guys she is texting there. If you don't want to wait until that point to request her number, you can also request her phone number to continue a better conversation off the platform.

You alive? Lol

Oh I am sorry I am almost never on here

Yeah me neither, let's talk on WhatsApp, it is more reliable. What's your number.

Regardless if you want to wait until the soft close or want to ask for her number to continue a conversation, she needs to be invested first, at least a little bit, to give out her phone number. You should not encounter much resistance if you do it this way. You may not get compliance if you ask the number too soon when she hasn't been investing in the conversation much. To get compliance, you need investment first; remember that.

How to

Flirt Effectively:

Flirting thru text is an art, and there are a lot of different ways you can do it. Something significant is how you start to flirt and in what context you are doing it. The good thing about it is that sometimes it is okay to be a bit random. First, I want you to know that you should not lead the conversation by validating her. I know I said this a lot already, but sometimes you need to repeat things: She needs to earn your validation by her investing in the conversation. Do not flirt with her when she is not being compliant with you. Otherwise, you are validating her non-compliance. You always want to find and use the opportunities you have, or she gives you to insert a creative flirty text

If you are going to send a flirty text, avoid typing super long text. Keep it short, sexy, and classy. You want to inject sexual tension and fun into your conversations. When flirting, you will compliment her mildly and in a non-thirsty way. It is different than when you are sexting. Be calm, cool, and classy.

Keeping it nonthirsty is a lot more attractive to them than the drooling texts, at least at the beginning. Remember, the key to flirting over text is to keep it light, playful, and fun. Avoid being overly aggressive or sexual; leave that when you are sexting the girl. The right words will depend on your relationship and the individual you're flirting with, so it's important to tailor your messages to the situation.

Playfully

<u>Misinterpret What She Says:</u>

You can use some things she says where it is obvious that is not what she meant to say, but you purposefully misinterpret to move the conversation into a more fun and flirty direction. Here is where you have to use your creativity a bit. Do not be looking over for this all the time, but when you see an opportunity, use a text of hers to playfully tease her and add sexual tension to the conversation. Do it in a calibrated way so that it doesn't come up to strong.

<u>Take a look at this example:</u>

The goal is to move the conversation in a sexual direction by using her own words. Use whatever she is saying inside the conversation and flip it into something funny and playful. This spices up the conversation, making it less generic and bland. A lot of men are masters in making conversations boring. Women want to be excited. Also, do not overthink it; flow with it, if you overthink everything too much, you will mess up. Have fun with it; the more you practice it, the better you will do it like anything in life. Don't take it too seriously. Make her feel good and comfortable.

There is a fine line between flirting and being a creep. There is no perfect thing to say just don't pester, and avoid cliches as well; most girls consider them boring.

Flirt Confidently:

It can be exciting to text a girl you like, but you need to maintain your frame as a high-value man. Do not show desperation or over-excitement when you are texting her. Women find it very attractive when a man can talk and flirt with them in a non-thirsty, classy way.

Seems you already do

You dont need keys to drive me crazy

Do you have a name or I can call you mine

I am a thief, I am here to steal your heart

They find that very attractive that you a comfortable enough in your own skin to tease her because you like her. If you do it this way, she is less likely to get offended and more likely to catch on to your humor.

Flirting may lead to sexting; if you see that the conversation keeps escalating, maintain your composure and do not lose control of yourself. A common mistake guys make is when things start getting a little sexual, they go from 0 to 100 real quick. Do not get overly excited if a conversation is going well. If you lose it, you will come off as immature and uncalibrated. Keep it together. It doesn't mean that you do not have to talk sexually; it just means not jumping over if you are not here yet.

Girls like it with men can openly talk about all kinds of things without losing their cool. We will talk more on to sexualize effectively in chapter 6.

Use the "we frame":

Using you and her as an entity can be powerful when trying to flirt with a girl. Talk about both of you when you are referring to things like events that you can do together or situations you are involved in or picturing something in her mind with you.

"We" are going to do this.

"We" are going to be that couple/ We, us together; you want to use those words with her.

Playfully Teasing her:

Women secretly love being teased. It brings all kinds of emotions. Teasing is an important part of seduction. If you do it correctly, you can create immense attraction. It is easier to do it than you think. There are a lot of different ways you can tease a girl, and it all depends on the level of trust you have with her. Just to give you ideas, I'll give you a few ways that you can playfully tease.

- Joke about her habits
- Make fun of her for making a mistake
- You can disagree with something she says
- You can accuse her of hitting on you
- You can challenge her
- Give her nicknames
- You can treat her like a child
- You can roleplay with her
- You can mimic or mock her
- You can purposefully misinterpret what she says

Teasing is a way of humorous flirtation. Try to leave space for her to tease you back and ensure it doesn't come off as you insult her. The idea is to make her laugh and spark attraction. Teasing shows confidence and that you are not afraid to play with her a little bit, and you are not putting her on a pedestal because teasing is a signal you are not scared to push her away. But, of course, that is not the intention.

<u>Another Example:</u>

Do not cross boundaries, and don't be inappropriate. Especially if you just met the girl, you need to know where you are with her and where the line is and not suddenly cross that line. Do not say things about her physical appearance, family, or something very personal. This is what you know she would not be comfortable with. There is a fine line between teasing and critiquing or negging. It will come off as super cringe and get the woman away from you.

Example:

It's important to never cross the line from teasing to bullying or harassment. Be respectful of the girl's boundaries and never say or do anything that makes her feel uncomfortable or threatened.

If she feels like you are attacking her or insulting her, it will not end well for you, she will get turned off, and that will be the end of the conversation.

How to

Ask Her Out and Close:

Most guys struggle with this. They may manage to get the girl to talk to them, but they cannot get a girl to meet up with them. Most of the time it is because you are either asking her out randomly when she hasn't been investing much in the conversation or you are not following a process correctly or jumping steps. The first rule is to get the girl invested in the conversation first, at least a little, before going for the meetup. If you ask her out without her being invested in you, you are making it easy for her to say no.

The more she invests in the interaction, the less likely she will reject your proposal and be more compliant with whatever plans you propose, instead of asking her out when she did not invest much in the conversation. It doesnt mean you have to wait a month to ask her out; it will depend on how long it takes you to get a conversation flowing. Just make sure you don't do it too soon because if you do, she will be less likely tor to flake on you if she does comply.

Once you have some investment, you have to go for a soft close. You will introduce the idea of meeting up, and you are not proposing a date, time, or activity yet. Your goal is to get her to agree that a meetup should happen.

<u>Examples of this are:</u>

We should get together sometime soon
We should celebrate
We should do this or that sometime soon
I'd like to get together sometime soon

The idea is for her to agree that you should both meet. Another way is you can ask her if she likes a certain drink, place, or activity, and once you get a positive response, you can introduce the idea of doing that together.

<u>Examples of this are:</u>

Do you like wine? We should split a bottle sometime soon
Do you like (X place) ? W should go together sometime

Have you ever done this or that?

We should do this or that

Once you get to this point, you will figure out her schedule. You want to get a feel of her routine and when she'll be free and convenient for her to meet with you so you can lock up a date and time.

<u>Different ways for you to do this:</u>

When are you available next

Are you usually free on weekdays or weekends

How's this weekend looking for you?

Where do you live?

What's your schedule like

This is crucial on the first date with a girl. You want to make sure things are clear when doing logistics.. It is much easier to meet up randomly and spontaneously later in the relationship but not on the first date; you want to follow up on these steps. A common mistake guys make here is that they don't know the girl's schedule and propose a random date and time.

<u>Example:</u>

She may be willing to go out with you, but she cannot do it in that specific date and time that you are saying. Like this, you are making it easy for her not to comply with you.

From the last example, adding that step, the conversation will look a bit different.

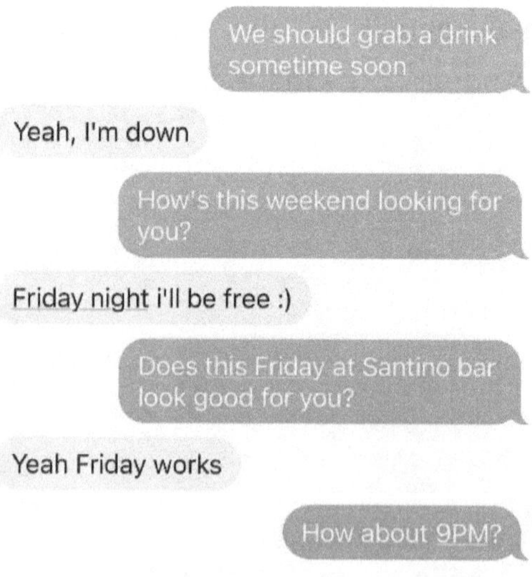

Once you know, you will propose a specific date and time that you will meet, also called a hard close. If you are in sales, you will find this process very familiar. Doing it this way increases your chances of her complying with you, accepting your idea for an activity, and making a date more solid. She is less likely to flake on you. Once you know what day she will be free, you are ready to do the hard close. Now you are ready to lock down a date in time. DO NOT ask her what she would like to do or where she would like to go. You are the man, and you have to come up with the activity. Women expect you to lead and for you to decide where to go and what to do.It is up to you want you want to do. You may want to ask her straight to your place or meet at some bar. It will depend of how far you can take her with her.

Confirming the date:

After you set up the date, typically, people set up the date a few days in advance. From there on, you don't need to keep texting a lot until the day of the day, but simultaneously, you want to keep the communication warm.

Let's say you set up the day on a Tuesday to meet up on Saturday night. There is no reason to be texting back and forth a lot until then. But you need to confirm the date; you cannot just take for granted that the girl will meet up with you. The way you will do it is the day before the date, in this case, Friday, you will open her up and have a little conversation with her. In that conversation, you can assume the day will happen by giving statements. An example of that would be

One of the ways to do is to assume it will happen. Do not start the text asking her right away is she is ok with the date

Don't confirm that way. Assume that it will happen by a statement instead of asking if it will happen. When you do it this way, you can assure more that the date will happen and you will communicate to her that you will make it as well as decrease your chances of her flaking on you. The conversation the day prior doesn't need to be that long, either.

On the day of the date, you can re-engage the conversation like 3-4 hours before, and here yes, you can be more straightforward and ask her if she is still good for the date.

Once you open her, You can say things like:

See you at 9?
Still good for tonight?
Would you like me to pick up for later?

It will not always be this easy. You are still at risk that something can come up that she will flake on you, she needs to reschedule, or she will give you objections. But following these steps, the likelihood of a girl flaking on you will dramatically decrease. You have to have the odds in your favor.

What to do
<u>When She Flakes On You:</u>

The best way to deal with flaking is to do the best you can to avoid it from happening in the first place. The best way to avoid it is to build investment. It is possible that you can set a date with a girl investing that was investing very little in the conversation, but the chances of her flaking on you will be higher compared to the girl investing paragraphs into the conversation. Maybe you were sexting each other or you talked on the phone a little bit. You want to get her invested emotionally, sexually, or intellectually in the conversation and combine it with proper scheduling to avoid flaking from happening. Then make sure you set up the date on a day when she will be free; you don't want her to squeeze you in or see you on a time restriction. You want to make sure she doesn't have much going on other than to see you; this will make a date a lot more solid.

Following this process will minimize the chances of the girl flaking on you in the first place, but it is not a guarantee it can still happen, and you have to deal with the situation in the most optimal way possible. Now, why she flaked on you? Does it matter? It does a little because the reason tells you if she is or not is interested in meeting up. It can be several different reasons, and you will never know exactly the reason at the moment; you only have what she is telling you and how she is reacting.

The most common reasons are:

- She really did not feel well
- She got too nervous about seeing you
- A legitimate emergency came
- She is in a different emotional state than when she texted you
- She chooses to do something more familiar with her over you
- She has concerns or objections she didn't have earlier
- She went to see another guy

There are a lot of other reasons as well that she could flake. It can be about you or not about you; it is up to you to find out. It could be that she simply had a change of heart or that something came up that was out of her control. Maybe it doesn't have anything to do with you at all. Rather than getting upset, try to communicate with her calmly and understanding to get a better idea of what happened. You could also use this opportunity to set boundaries and make it clear that you expect her to follow through on her commitments in the future.

Your reaction will say a lot to her about you. So what you don't want to do is to respond emotionally, get butthurt, angry, or needy. Be understanding of the situation and do your best to reschedule.

From that example, she flaked on him but also made an effort to reschedule the date. A very important detail about a girl flaking on you is the way she does it. If she seem sorry and still shows interest in seeing you or not putting any effort into rescheduling, and she doesnt seem to feel bad about it.

Like is this example, he texted her the day before the meeting with, "Hey trouble maker". She did not respond to that, which was not a good sign. On the day of the date, he asked her if they were still on for the date, and she just said she is not feeling well, was not very apologetic, and did not put any effort into rescheduling. Here is a situation where you have to do a bit of digging and find out the situation with her. Do not reward flaky behavior by you investing more in the conversation. Just show that you are disappointed by pulling back a bit.

When you get low-investment texts like that where she is canceling on you, it doesn't make that much sense to reschedule right there since she is flaking and giving you a low investment and doesnt seem to feel bad about flaking on you. In situations like that, it is best to ask what happened; maybe she will tell you, and you will have a better idea of where you stand with her and if it is still possible to get the meetup. If it is, you have to follow the same process and get her to invest in the conversation and go for the meeting again in the near future.

You have to screen out the girls you are texting not to waste your time, especially girls you get from dating apps that are only there for attention and validation. They will not be interested in meeting up, and even if you have done all the steps correctly, they will not meet with you. You will show understanding and tolerance the first time she flakes, but if she keeps doing it you want to call out her behavior.

Call her out:

I want to be clear about this. You want to do this as a last resort. If you do this too early on, it may backfire on you. You have to use it once you have used all other resources first, and you have not been needy, but she is not budging. She either flaked on you more than once or you know that she is purposefully not responding and doesn't tell you what's happening. You are trying to find out the reason why she is behaving that way. This needs to be done in a nonaggressive and non-butthurt way.

Maybe it is something related to you: This applies to a girl you know a bit more. Perhaps you have been talking with her for a while, or a girl you are already in a relationship with, or you slept with her already. If she was investing in the conversation before, but she no longer is. Something happened, either related or unrelated to you. An underlying concern or objections or maybe something you did or something that happened in her life. Sometimes you have to dig to find out what that reason is if you don't know it. Maybe at the time of the meeting, she is not responding to you because she is nervous about meeting you. Use your senses, you should have an idea of your situation. What are you perceiving? You have to find out by calling her out if she doesn't tell you because many times they won't

<u>There are different texts you can use to call out a girl when she has had a repeated history of being flakey:</u>

- Are you always this difficult to make plans with
- Would you tell me what's up
- Let me know if you are not into this so I can stop trying
- May I know what's on your mind
- I genuinely didn't take you for the flakey type
- Is there a reason you are playing these silly games

It also needs to be done appropriately for the situation; it cannot seem from an angry or butthurt.

You are just pointing out her behavior from an emotionally neutral standpoint. A callout text would look something like

"Love the enthusiasm!" That is the call out for that text. You are basically saying. Woow, are you this disinterested in seeing me? You are not putting up with this like that.

Another callout example. Let's say that you have been texting each other for months, she has been flakey with seeing you, but she is still responding to you.

<u>After months of texting and inviting her out ..</u>

Remember that the goal of texting is to get the meetup with her, so when you first start texting, and you start to build investment, you have to make moves to the meetup. It is absolutely pointless to talk only and never see each other. Some studies have shown that people who have been texting a lot before meeting up did not hit off that well in person. Build and then go for the meetup. It is entirely ok to reschedule sometimes; things happen she may flake on you; you out her behavior.

With a good callout text and some sarcasm, you can turn things around sometimes; she will see you as a man who will not put up with that behavior. Also, a good callout text may get the girl to tell you the concern or objection, allowing you to address it and move things forward.

This will likely happen on the first few dates and if you invite her to your place. Keep in mind that she will be nervous and needs to feel safe to go out and meet you. So if she tells you a concern or objection, address it.

How to pass her shit tests:

Women will always test you, consciously or subconsciously, and they will do it over text as much as they do in person. Women do this naturally and often don't even realize that they are doing it.

Another way people call a shit test is a "congruence test".

First, what is a shit test? Simply, it is an intentional challenge or provocation that a woman puts on a man to see what kind of man they are with, what he's made of. Is it a tool that she uses to evaluate you and see if you are worthy of a sexual partner, or a relationship or even to know if they should keep the conversation going forward. As I said before, most of the time, women do this unintentionally and subconsciously. One reason they do this is that they are very used to men pretending to be one way, and when they get to know them, they are different. Most women went thru the experience of dating a man portraying himself as the alpha male guy who makes all this money, and he has his shit together when they turn out to be a complete fraud.

So she is looking to figure out who you are as a person and to see if she should let her guard down with you. So a lot of the time, it isn't so much about you. It is about what they have been thru.

They are different ways women can shit test you, like purposely flaking on you, testing your compliance to see if you do what she says, asking for favors, challenging you with something specific to test your reaction and how congruent you are, etc. It isn't easy to name them all because they do it in many ways. Sometimes, whatever the situation is, they will find the moment to test your manhood when an opportunity arises.

When it comes to shit tests thru text, they look something like this.

- You say this to every girl, don't you?
- Is this the process you use on every girl?
- You meet a lot of girls don't you?
- You know I am not going to have sex with you right?
- Maybe if you're lucky will do this or that
- Do you say that to every girl?
- You are not going to open the door for me?
- You are not going to buy that for me?
- I am coming with a friend, do you mind?
- You just want to get me drunk and sleep with me dont you?
- Is that your idea for a date?
- Are you calling me (Fill in the blank)?
- Ohh I am just your booty call now?
- Can we meet at a bar instead?
- Do you really expect me to come to your place at the first meet?
- You are not going to buy me a drink?
- Do you mind if I'm going to be with friends?
- What would you do if I do (Fill in the blank) to you?

You know where I am going, and you have probably dealt with situations like this before. It will be a lot easier to pass her shit test thru text than in person since when she is texting you, you have time to think about your response as opposed to where you are in person; you have seconds to react, and you may do the wrong thing. Passing her tests is not complicated; most tests will be challenges so passing her shit tests is about maintaining your frame and not being a pushover. Do not be afraid to say no, and have boundaries. They are so many different types of tests she can do on you, and they can be flattery, silly, playful, sometimes she will be just trolling you, and tests that you can laugh it out, have fun and play around with, other tests can be more challenging or maybe ask you to do something you don't want to do. Others can be justflat-out disrespectful, and you should not tolerate things like that. You have to be socially calibrated and take it where it came from.

Shit tests are easy to identify and to pass, and for most cases, there will be no reason to be mad, offended, or butthurt: if you get

If you see from that example, she says to him that he is all about sex, the wrong way to respond would have been TO BE apologetic and say something like:

"No it is really not like that"
"Sorry it it came up that way, I swear I am not"

But he did the right way; he got playful with her, took it with humor and sarcasm. Women want to be with a man that isn't afraid to stand out to them, men with backbone.

The best way to deal with many of the shit tests is to get playful and sarcastic.

Compliance test:

Sometimes women will test you, giving you commands to see if you obey them at your own expense. She typically to this to see how much you can stand to your principles or if you are the typical "Yes" man who agrees with everything she says and do everything she wants. This is a nice guy trait; they just cannot say no to women.

There will be a lot of this dominance shit test when a girl tells you to do something for her where you have to get out of your way. If what she is asking is inconvenient for you. Do not fall for it. Respectfully decline.

Dominance tests:

These are the type of tests where she wants to see who wears the pants in the relationship. She will sometimes do something almost disrespectful to test your reaction and see if you have frame control.

With silly shit tests, they are not a big deal. Be unreactive, and don't let them get to you. Troll her back and see this as a good thing, since it means she is considering you for something. If she wasn't doing things like this, she doesnt seem to be considering you for a relationship or yourself, also, you do not get easily offended and upset. You are not getting defensive all the time with her, and you are not showing insecurities when she challenges you about a specific thing

You pass them this way by showing emotional intelligence, which is a characteristic of a high-value man. You can maintain your composure and have control of your situations and circumstances.

Another way you can deal with a shit this is to agree and exaggerate:

When she throws you a random accusation or challenge to you like that, you can just agree and playfully exaggerate with it. It will immediately show your sense of humor and help alleviate any tension that question probably brought.

Also, you can try to flip whatever she is saying back to her.

If she teases you or trolls you like that, it is a great opportunity to do it back to her, and this also makes her think twice before trolling you like that. Not always for every situation you have to be dismissive, playful or unreactive. There will be situations where you are going to deal with disrespect sometimes. When that happens,act accordingly.

In almost every situation, passing shit tests comes from frame control, strength, and character. This type of test are normal and they will come not only from women you are romantically involved with but also from a manager, family members, friend, colleagues, etc. You cannot control when or how it happens; you can only control how you react to them. Identify them and act accordingly. The worst thing you can do is start explaining yourself, respond emotionally, take it personally, get angry or start giving excuses when the situation doesnt call for it. But also be open to constructive criticism. it is not about being arrogant.

Another example:

From those examples, guys reacted softly and apologetically when they didn't need to. That is the worst reaction you can have; it shows the girl that you are too compliant with her and have no backbone. You will not be able to react positively in every situation in person, but when it comes to texting, you can almost always pass them if you can identify them and think about your response. This requires a lot of practice and takes time to respond naturally. Your competence will determine your confidence. Keep it to the basis and maintain your cool attitude, don't lose it when you don't have to. As you see, it will always come back to frame control.

Texting her

After The First Date:

How you text her after the first date will vary significantly depending on how the date went. If the date went poorly, you must keep doing most of the initiating and pursuing. If the date went well, she should start investing a bit more so you can pursue her a little less. If you were able to get physical with her, kiss her, or even better, you had sex with her, here is a situation where you can back off a bit, give her space and let her chase. If the date did not go that well, meaning the connection wasn't there that much, and you feel like she was not into you, you will have to keep pursuing the work of getting her to invest and raise her level of interest if you want to see her again. There are ways to redeem yourself for a date that did not go as planned. Test the waters and find out how she felt about the date with you, and you will be able to feel her vibe to see if she is interested in meeting you again or not.

Ask yourself. How did the date go? Did you have fun together? Did she like your vibe? Was it flirting involved? Were you able to see she was interested in you sexually? Did you talk with her about meeting again? If not, would she be interested in meeting you again? Something good to do is to bring ideas at the end of the date of activities to do next time if everything is going well up to that point.

Instead of texting her if she got home ok, it is better to let her know in advance to text you when she gets home and wait for that text. If you have to ask her, that's fine. Ask her if she got home ok and go along with her level of investment. Close the conversation and do not text her for 2-3 days to see if she would initiate on you.

You might be surprised, she may initiate the conversation with you if the date went well.

You know how the date went and how you should proceed. The worst mistake you want to make is getting impatient, and chasing to see her again. Remember that at the beginning, you just want to see her once, maybe twice a week. Your goal is to keep her interested for her to want to see you again. Do what feels natural to you but do not show that you are crazy for her.

Be patient, do not rush things, go along with your life and keep being mysterious and unpredictable.

You are trying to facilitate her being comfortable with you. If the date went well, she should invest more in the conversation and make it easier for both of you to meet again. She may sometimes initiate if you give her space and time.

I cannot give you examples of what to text after the first date since it will vary significantly. If it went well, go a bit easier on the pursuing and let her come to you; keep the conversations to a minimum only to sext and set up the next encounter. If things did not go that well, you might still need to do most of the pursuing and initiating, but it doesn't need to go over the top.

Texting Her

<u>After You Sleep With Her For The First Time:</u>

First of all, good job, You slept with her, which means that she has a high level of interest in you, and you have been doing most things right, so great job there. If everything went great, the sex, the connection, and the night was positive. Now it is time to relax and back off a bit. Here it is when you have to give her time to miss you and give her space to pursue you. It is time for her to put a little bit of work. Of course, this assumes everything went well, and you want to see her again.

Give her space and let her mind race about you. After having sex with her, try not to text her for 2-3 days to see if she initiates a text with you. If she doesn't, you can initiate. If you think we are playing mind games, women play games on men all the time, and it is totally accepted in society, it is ok for men to play their cards as well. You want to keep the level of interest after sex. I am not saying you have to disappear for a whole week or not respond to her messages. If she texts you, reply, of course. Have a short conversation with her. Maybe talk about your next encounter and sext a little, but give her space to pursue you. If you are too available, always there, initiating and pursuing, she will not do it because you always do it. Once you do this and plan the next date, get off the phone. It feels great when a woman pursues you.

Respecting The Stages of

<u>Where You Are With The Women:</u>

You need to be self-aware of where you are with every woman you interact with. Many men make the mistake of being too impulsive, just saying whatever comes to mind, and sometimes being out of context. It is entirely different texting a woman you just met to a woman you are in a relationship with. Act accordingly, depending on the stage that you are with her. We are going to recap the process

Simple opener/ Start the conversation:

Keep it simple and to the point. Avoid using long openers, being overly wordy, or using pickup lines. It comes off as really low value

Build investment: Have some back-and-forth texts and get her to talk to you. You are not asking for the meetup without her investing in the conversation a little bit. Make her comfortablewith you and try to flirt with her as well.

Take your chances to sexualize: If you see an opportunity to add sexual tension to the conversation, try and take it. Remember you are starting slow and testing the waters to build it from there.

Be patient, pursue, but don't chase: The timeframes to get a date from when you started talking with her can vary. It can be a few days to a few weeks. Depending on how long it takes you to get her to invest. Be patient and take your time, keep building investment, and double text correctly. DO NOT CHASE. You have to wait until you have some investment to a soft close.

Be on your purpose: While doing this, you are not supposed to make this your primary focus. While you wait to text her, you are not looking at the calendar and looking at the time. Get busy and work on your life objective while you do this. It will be a lot easier for you.

Do a soft close: Once you have some investment go for it. Introduce the idea of meeting with her and get her to agree. The more investment you could build in the conversation, the more compliant she will be.

Figure out her schedule: Get a feel of her schedule and routine to see when she'll be free so you can go for the hard close.

Do the hard close: Once you know the dates, she'll be free. Do the hard close. You are the one who chooses the place and activity

Confirm correctly: This is a crucial step. If you do not confirm correctly, the date may not happen. The date before the date open her, chats a bit and assume with that the date will happen. On the date of the date, text her 2-3 hours before for another confirmation.

Prepare yourself for successful dates: This book is mainly about texting but prepares you before meeting her. Look your best and act your best. If you have successful dates with her, you should be hooking up by the second or third date. If both of you guys vibe, there is a good connection, and after the third date, you keep seeing her once a week or more. Here it is when you can back off a little bit and let her do most of the texting, chasing, and pursuing. If she likes you and you keep dating her, she should invest more in the conversation if you give her space. The hardest part is done. Now you decide if you want to keep going into a deeper relationship with her.

CHAPTER 5

HOW TO BE PERSISTENT WITHOUT BEING NEEDY

A lot of men need help finding a balance here. They want to push, but at the same time, they don't want to seem clingy, needy or desperate. How do I do this? You probably asked yourself this before. Keep something in mind. Being needy will turn most girls off, but persistence will show a woman that you have the balls to go after what you want, and that turns most girls on. So let's talk about how to be persistent without being needy.

There isn't a way around it.

In the beginning, you have to do most of the work:

There is no secret that she will be the least invested in the conversation at the first stages of the interaction, so this process will apply mainly at the beginning when getting the girl into going to the first and second dates with you. She doesn't know you yet, her texts will be short, and sometimes she will not even reply to you depending on the circumstance. So you will have to persist thru that. One of the reasons why it is hard to get their attention is because their experience with the opposite sex is entirely different from our experience. As I said before, they get bombarded with texts from different guys, so much of the low investments comes from this reason.

So to persist without being needy is to pursue without chasing. You have to keep working on building investment, but when she doesnt respond for one reason or another, follow up and double-text strategically in a way that it doesn't get you into the chasing category. The hottest girls will give the most work. There will be cases where it will take you weeks, maybe even months, to get a date with a girl. and those sometimes end up turning into the best hookups or relationships. If you are a busy man who is on his purpose and you have a life, you don't see this as a problem because you are busy with your life, and whenever both of your schedules can match up you'll meet, not a big deal. That is the mindset you want to have. If you react negatively and are not patient, that comes with a scarcity mindset, and you have to work on that.

Another big sign of neediness is impatience. Like you can't help yourself, you are always texting her and looking forward for to her text you back. And if she doesn't you double text, quadruple text. This is so common. Be talking and dating different women. Do not get obsessed over just one girl. Having success with texting and dating has a lot to do with your mindset and what you do with your life. So you introduce this while you are working in the lifestyle you want. It is a lot less work than you think; You have to do your thing and let time, patience, and persistence do their job.

How to

Double Text Effectively:

The main form of persistence you will be doing is double texting. Which is totally okay in the right context, and it is terrible in the wrong context. When you double-text, the right way is persistence, and the wrong way is neediness.

The secret of double texting is that it is okay to do it depending on the time you take to send the follow-up text, the context of the situation, and the text itself. It is different from double texting just a few hours later with a needy text as to waiting 2-3 days to double text with a non-needy text.

Assuming you are not in a time-sensitive situation with her, you should wait 2-3 days from the last text to re-engage. You go, do your thing, work on your goals, and if you see that after three days, if she does not reply, then follow up. When you re-engage, you can do two things: Follow up on what was said in the text before or reopen and start a new conversation. It will depend on the context and the conversation you were having.

There are a million different reasons why a girl may not text back. This will happen more at the beginning of your interaction. She may have low to medium interest. Do not lose your shit when she doesnt respond; text and forget and work on whatever you have going on.

Here is an example of timing and following up.

Wait 2-3 days, and then follow up on your last text.

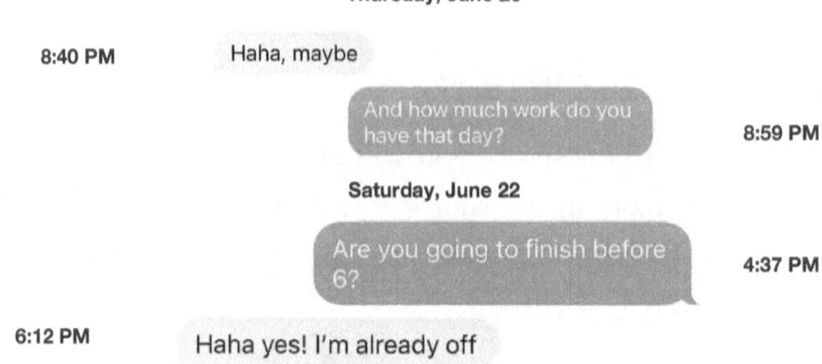

From that example, they were having a normal conversation, and she just stopped replying. The reason in this case, is irrelevant. Thursday, June 20 was the last text; he waited two days and double-texted on Saturday, June 22, following up on the previous text. Double texting this way is entirely different than double or triple texting after a few hours go by.

Another example:

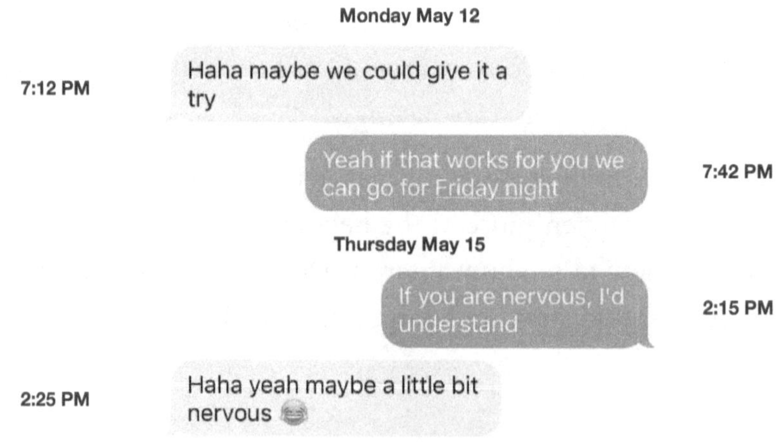

A very similar situation from this example, they were talking about meeting up, he didn't do anything wrong from the last text, and she didn't reply. It was a Monday he waited until Thursday to text her back with a follow-up text from the previous conversation.

The time you take to follow up and double-text will make the difference between chasing and pursuing. The wrong way to double text is after a few hours when there is no time constraint and you are getting t to know each other.

This is a clear example of neediness. You are too impatient; you cannot wait for her to respond.

If you see, he proposed the meeting that same night, and she wasn't available. He responds right back with, "Oh, Okay, maybe tomorrow". That right there is a ba,d text, showing that he is too impatient to meet up; he wants to get a date out of her right away and he is too available. A better way to follow up in a situation like that is to ask her what she would be doing that night and then flow the conversation and try to figure out a different day. Not only the last text comes off as really needy and low value, but only 3 hours later, he doubles text, and one hour later, he asks her why she is not responding. Huge mistake, and a lot of guys do this. Be patient, work on yourself, and then re-engage the conversation 2-3 days later if there is no time constraint. Everyone has a life, and you should have one. You need to text and forget. Combining timing with proper follow-up changes how you reappear in the scene. The reason why you want to wait 2-3 days is that you want to give her time to reply if she has the intention to. You will sometimes see that she will eventually reply if you have given her time or if she really likes you and she perceives you as a high-value man who doesn't chase her when she doesn't respond, which also motivates her to reply to you.

In the context where you have done nothing wrong and socially, you need a response.

Following up again to get that response is fine.

She told him she had a dream about him, and he asked her what the dream was about, but she did not reply; he waited three days and re-engaged with a follow-up message seeking that response.

Also, in the context where you are in a time-sensitive situation like meeting up, for example. It is okay to double-text.

Do not jump to conclusions if she doesn't reply to your last message. Stay positive and busy with your life. Stay patient, and do not second-guess yourself. Remember that everyone has a life, a schedule, things to do, places to go, work, school, etc. Distract yourself and do not be waiting by the phone. Have a life, text, and forget. That's how you get replies. Expect her to respond later when you are not that important in her life. You should be texting less at the first stages anyways since you are using texting mainly to make in-person plans. Save serious and deep conversations when you meet her in person. Keep it light to ensure things move at a healthy pace. The worst thing you can do is text her why she's not responding or seeking her validation just a few hours after your last message.

You should only double-text a girl when it is strategically likely to work in your favor, and time and context will make the difference between being neediness and persistence. She will find it attractive that you are comfortable in your own skin, did not lose your cool, and you are interested in her, and this behavior gets her to reciprocate.

Sometimes. YOU Be the one who doesn't text her back.

How to Do It Effectively:

You may be scared to do this because you probably never done it before. I know what you may be thinking.

Having this mentality is so beta. The majority of these concerns are invalid, and you are looking at it from a scarcity mindset. Don't think it that way. In the right context, when a guy doesn't reply to a text, that gets a woman's attention because she is not used to it; almost every guy they are talking to responds to every single text they send. Women are used to men always being available and excited to talk to them. When you are the guy that is not thirsty, not always available, not texting so much, and don't reply to them sometimes. That increases your perceived value in their eyes, and it makes you stand out from the crowd. If you do it correctly, it is an excellent trick that makes women notice you more, wonder about you, and get them to pursue your validation. It has happened to me many times before that I am talking to women just having a conversation, I get busy with my things, and I forget that I am talking to them, and all of the sudden, I see them double texting and pursuing me. Sometimes you may not respond because you are busy, you are a high-value man, your time is valuable, and you have things going on. She will appreciate your time more and makes your texts more valuable. Now I want to be clear about this. It will only work on girls who are invested in the interaction and have medium to high interest in you. If she is not, it may not work because she is not that invested in you just yet. You want to do this with girls invested in the conversation; maybe you have already slept with her, gone out on a few dates, or have been texting each other for a while. If you do it in the wrong

106

context, it can backfire. If her level is medium to high, you can try it to see how it works. Liking her message can also be a good strategy. You can only do that if you have an iPhone. You may be doing it sometimes because you are legitimately busy, which is okay. There are different ways to do this in the right way and also in the wrong way. Avoid this when you are sexting her, having engaging conversations, or working on logistics to meet up. Do it more when you are busy, do not feel like continuing a conversation, she responded with a low-investment text or you already have a date set up.

You can use this mostly when she is not investing in the conversation; if you do not want to respond to a text when you know the conversation is not going anywhere, try it as well. You may be surprised by the number of girls that would double-text you.

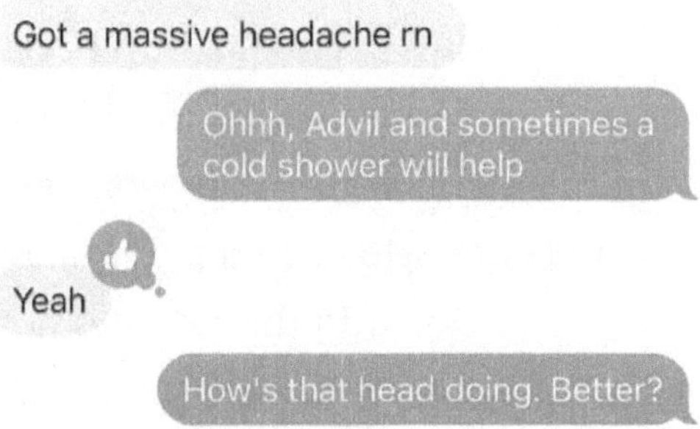

There is really no risk that you are taking with this. If this doesnt get her to reply, reopen the conversation again two or three days later, you are not double texting her; you are just responding to her. Another time you shouldn't feel bad about not replying is if you don't feel like it. If you have a stressful day, you are hustling at work, and you don't feel like keeping the conversation or pursuing her, don't text her back. Do not feel obligated to respond to every single text she sends you. If you are in your mission and your purpose in life, you will do this naturally. Little by little, you will see women investing in the conversation a little more. After all, it is not all about them; you respond when you can because you are legitimately busy.

Women are used to them being the ones leaving guys on read. Once you do this, you will stand out because you are not like every other guy that is blowing up her phone. She will wonder what you are doing and why you are not texting her back, and she will start doubting herself with you. You don't want her to be so sure about you, and you want her to doubt a little bit where she stands with you. As I said before, it is scientifically proven that women are more attracted to men whose feelings are unclear.

When to move on:

You know when you need to move on when you are already chasing the woman. If you are triple-quadruple texting her, and she would not invest in the conversation, maybe she is straight up ignoring you. It is time to move on. When you keep insisting and it is clear that she is not interested in you, and maybe she told you that, but you keep going. Don't do that. It does not help your case. Stop everything and move on to the next girl. There is no reason to keep pursuing something with her when is clearly not going anywhere. Do not be another beta male orbiter. Most women have too many of them already. You are moving on if you see that she is not into you and not investing in the conversation whatsoever, even though you have been trying to get her to invest for a while. When you see that is not pursuing anymore, it is chasing; move on. I don't want you to be giving up too soon as well. If she still engages and replies to some of your messages and accepts the general idea of meeting with you, but it still doesn't happen, there is something in there to keep pursuing. Try calling out her behavior. She needs to give you something to work with if she doesn't for a long time. Do not continue. If you see that the pursuit turns into chasing, that is the time to move on.

CHAPTER 6

SEXUALIZING AND SEXTING

Sexualizing with a woman comes from starting slowly and building it little by little. It is a way to build sexual tension, and if you get her to respond and play along with sexting, that means that she is into you, and sex is likely to happen in your next encounter with her.

This is something that most guys struggle with. Maybe they are able to get the girl to be down to sext with them, but then they end up turning the girl off and pushing her away. They are not able to keep a sexual conversation exciting; they turn themselves on, but they don't turn the girl on, and that's what you want to do.

I am going to give you some of the most common mistakes men make when trying to sexualize the conversation and ways to do it effectively so you can sext girls in a way to turn them on and makes them desire you sexually. The idea of sexting is to get the sexual tension going so you increase your chances of having sex with her when you see her next.

Mistake # 1

<u>Going 0 to 100 Real Quick:</u>

The most common mistake men make when attempting to sexualize the conversation is to jump into sending sexual texts out of the blue or go to the next level much quicker than they should.

They are having a back-and-forth chat with the women, and suddenly, they text something sexual or a lot more sexual than the prior text.

Do you really want to jump there?

Well, the best place for you to jump right now would be on my dick

Oh really..

If you look at that example, the prior conversation wasn' t sexual whatsoever. He suddenly and out of nowhere injected an intense sexualization into the conversation. This behavior will throw the girl off, and she will likely not respond to something like this. Women make fun of men who have this behavior, and it also implies that you have no control over yourself. You need to build the sexualization in the conversation little by little over time. You must see how willing she is to have a sexual conversation with you and build it from there. She never should feel like, "Where the F** this come from". One text should not be significantly different from another text.

<u>An example of that would be something like:</u>

What is something that you would like me to do?
What if i say kneel down and lowly unzip my pants?
I'll pull your pants down and rub the outside of your boxers
Slowly afterwards you can start pulling them down
I'll be exited to see what you packing

If you see that she is responding to your sexual intent, you can slowly build it and increase the sexual tension. Once you have momentum, it is not that hard to build it; don't make big jumps.

Women get turned on differently than guys. Think about it this way. Guys get turned on like a light switch. You see the woman, and you like her, you want to sleep with her" Women get turned on like a volume knob. You slowly increase the volume from 0 to 100, or like a bonfire, you have to create a spark and slowly grow the fire with sticks, twigs, and logs. If we try to jump too quickly into a sexual conversation, we will not achieve the girl of turning them on; we will actually turn her off.

When you see the conversation moving in a sexual direction, read her reaction, and adjust appropriately. If her response is positive, you are ok to keep going. Do not sexualize suddenly, and keep your composure. Act dominant, not thirsty, and do not escalate if she is not playing along with you. Be patient; all that dirty stuff that you want to tell her, you will be able to if you do it the right way; you need to build it a little bit first, especially if it is a girl that you are recently dating.

Mistake#2

<u>Not Sexualizing In A Way That Appeals To That Particular Woman:</u>

Every woman has a different taste in sex; some are more conservative than others. You cannot assume that the particular woman you are talking to will be into getting slapped in the face and fucked by the dumpster. Some will but not all. So if you sexualize in a particular way, she may not be into that. You have to start a bit more generally first, and then once you get to know her turns on then, you can get more specific. But guys make the mistake of sexualizing in a specific way sometimes, and it may or may not be appealing to that specific girl.

Every woman has her preferences. You must find the arousal to that particular woman you are talking to. And by following what I said before, which is not jumping around, you would be able to notice, and she may tell you as well. There are a few sexual triggers that arouse almost all women—things like intelligence, dominance, and assertiveness. Just don't get into specific ways of sexualization without first finding out what she likes. Start slow, build up and be careful of being too vulgar. Vulgarity is ok when you are in a deeper relationship with the woman and you already know her very well. Avoid it at first unless you see she is into it, and you can build slowly. Vulgarity is fine but save it more when you are having sex with her.

Mistake # 3

Sending A Picture of Your D Randomly:

This is something that a lot of guys do. They think a woman will enjoy a random picture of your d***, and she won't if you send it in the wrong context. Typically I do not recommend sending a picture of down there UNLESS she asks for it or you ask her if she would like one first. Make her earn it. Do not just give it away. Make her want to see it before you send it. Women do not get turned on so much visually as we do. She has to expect it. She will enjoy it more, and it will turn her on because you are sending it when she is expecting it and wishing for it.

Mistake#4

Long Sexting Paragraphs Giving It All Away:

We have all done this when we are having a sexual conversation. Not only do we jump into a more explicit sexualization, but we also do it by writing long paragraphs giving away all the process of what we would like to do to them.

Saying all of this is not bad, but saying it all together in this fashion. The girl feels just like, too much too soon. A text like that would have been much more powerful if you would break it into pieces and build it little by little. See how much she plays along with you and break it into 4 or 5 texts. So when you are sexualizing, and you have all of those things that you want to say to her, instead of texting all of it into one long paragraph, split it into a few different texts. It is a lot better to do it this way since her response may say something different where. You can follow up on it and have a better, more explicit, and exciting sexual conversation with her.

A better response to that text would have been something like

And then, depending of her response you keep building the tension..

There are some instances where the long process giveaway can work, but I found it to be a lot more effective to break it into pieces.

Why You Need To
<u>Position Yourself As A Sex Expert:</u>

When you position yourself as a sexual authority, that makes you stand out. Most guys are not good in bed, do not text or sexualize correctly and suck at turning a girl on. If she thinks you are the rare guy who knows what you are doing and how to fuck well. She will go out of her way to text and see you and see you.

So far, you see that the girl's concern is that she doesn't usually hook up on the first night of meeting someone and that she did not have the best experiences with sex. Most girls are in that boat. They were not fucked properly; they did not get turned on that much, and guys she thought would be good at seducing her and giving her a good experience turned out to be a big disappointment. Here the conversation continues with him positioning himself as the guy is not like that.

Implying that you are the exception and one of the few men who gets her will make you stand out, and she will be excited to see you. From that example, he positions himself as the teacher and her as the student. This is not the only way to do it; it was just an example. You have to use your creativity in a way that does for you. This has to be done smoothly, and if you can position it like this in her eyes, it will make your dates much more solid and sex more likely to happen by having a conversation like this. So when you can maintain your composure and talk about sex confidently and act like you are knowledgeable in the subject and are not scared to talk about it with them. This is a very attractive quality for women since they rarely find a guy that can do this. When you embrace your sexuality, she will embrace hers.

I am not saying you have to be overly respectful or politically correct or to treat her like a princess all the time, but if you move too fast, most of the time, it doesnt work very well; you have to be in CONTEXT. It will all depend on the relationship you have with that particular girl.

CHAPTER 7

DATINGS APPS

Where do I start? Dating apps are one of the main reasons for many of the dating problems we have in the first place. I am not going to tell you not to use them. But I will give you insights about them and why I am not a fan of using them as a guy, at least. If you have been using dating apps and don't find results and it seems like a waste of time, you are not alone, and it is not entirely your fault. Dating apps don't work for most men for multiple reasons. Standing out is challenging; the sad truth is that women get bombarded with messages from tons of different guys all the time. I am talking upwards of hundreds of messages from hundreds of different guys. So the odds of getting a girl to text exclusively with you more than other guys are very low to non-existent. You just become one man in a sea of men. Unless you are in the top 1 percent of men, it is tough to have success on them, and that's why I am not a fan of them because you can do everything right, have a great text game, a great profile,, and do everything that you are supposed to do and even though after all of that. You are still playing low odds. Dating apps are very superficial, and you have seconds to make a good impression. Standing out on a sea of thousands of messages and profiles is a daunting task few men are willing to take. You can do things to optimize your chances and increase your odds of getting a girl to notice you, but for many men, the efforts are not worth what they are getting out of them. Also, a large number of these women on dating apps, I would say about half are not there because they are interested in meeting a guy; they are using dating apps for validation and attention; they don't get there to find a partner or a guy to date. They get in there to get the ego boost of tons of men messaging them and trying to get with them. You also have many only fan girls that want to promote themselves. So not only are there more men than women on these apps, but also a large percentage of those women will be unqualified to date for something casual or a relationship, and you have to put some extra work screening them out on top of all the work it takes to have success on them. Don't get me wrong; you can use them and hook up with girls or find a relationship. Of course, it is, but it is also difficult.

The amount of messages these girls get on these apps is unbelievable, the game of datingapps is rigged against men and in favor of women, and it is hard for me to want to play a rigged game.

I am not saying that you cannot succeed with them, but you need to know that, unfortunately, the odds are against you, and you are playing a rigged game when using them. Many guys know this and are still willing to grind it out; some have succeeded, which is admirable. I have found more success on dating apps outside of the United States. The sexual marketplace on these apps is skewed, and if you decide to use them, you need to know what you are walking into because it can affect your self-esteem.

If you decide to give it a try to dating apps

Here Is What You Do:

Do you understand that dating apps will require much work and persistence?

Do you understand that it is a number's game?

Will you not take rejection personally?

The amount of time and energy it would take you as a man to have success on dating apps in western countries can be just as much as a part-time job, so if you still want to go ahead, let's grind it out.

Optimize your profile and pictures:

I will not get into the details of how to do this; many YouTube videos and internet articles can help you with this better than I do. But you have to treat dating apps as a sales funnel. If you ever work on internet marketing, a sales funnel is a process where you have a journey from a customer that doesnt know you until they buy from you. In your case, get a date with you.

Typically it goes from awareness, perceived value, interest, desire, and action. The product here is you. and women are the prospect. Women will be looking at your profile, so you must have good pictures of yourself showing an attractive lifestyle and a compelling description of yourself.

You need to have your perceived value as high as possible so that when you talk to girls on them, they are more likely to engage in a conversation with you.

It is a numbers game:

There is a lot of competition on these dating apps, so it is a numbers game you have to play.

You may have to talk to 50 women, so 10 of them can turn into a conversation, and five will turn into dates. And out of those, let's hope you can close 1 or 2.If you are in sales, you will find this very similar. If you go into this with this mindset, you will be more likely to have success with them than not knowing this and expecting to talk to 2 or 3 girls, and you will be able to get a date that easily. For women works that way but not for men. Give it a try and talk to at least 30 women to see how many of them turn into a date and see if it is worth the effort.

There are many dating apps out there; the most popular are Tinder, Bumble, Hinge, and Facebook Dating. They are all a little bit different, do your research in all of them and see which one would work for you. My least favorite one is Tinder it is the hardest to succeed. Bumble women text you first, so you don't waste too much time texting a bunch of women. Hinge is interesting; they advertised themselves as the only dating app meant to be deleted. They focus on actually helping both men and women find a partner. But users usually say it is just about the same as the others. Try them for yourself, get your own experience, and take your own conclusions.

If you decide to use dating apps, it is because you are aware of the work it will take. If you ask me, I would put this amount of time and energy into your business, hobbies, and whatever you are working on. But it is ok if you still want to experience them. Dating apps can take a toll on your self-esteem because the flake rate and the rejection you will encounter are very high, so be mentally prepared for them and don't take things personally. My suggestion is to experience them and see if they work for you and if you believe they are worth it. Go deep into them for maybe a month or two, do your best to optimize everything, and start messaging women. The messaging principles will be the same. Avoid long openers, keep things simple, build investment and get out of the platform as soon as possible. If you have an attractive profile, you will get matches; try to message all of those matches. Let's say that in a month, you can message 100 girls. Try to use the skills you learn with this book to see how many of those 100 conversations you initiated can turn into dates. Once you have played this for a while, you will decide whether they are worth your time.

If you decide not to use dating apps:

First, do not feel like you are making a bad decision by not using them; having success with dating apps is a daunting task and requires a lot of work, and you may not have the time or the energy to do this. And this is a good thing because it shows that you have something going on in your life, whether is your job, business, career, hobbies, interests, or goals. For a generation of people who have grown up with this as the norm and mainly use the internet to get to know people, they may find that impossible but remember, dating apps have only evolved and started becoming mainstream in the last 10-15 years. Match.com came in 1995, but people rarely used them. Tinder and Hinge were released in 2012, and from there, they have started to become more and more popular, so dating apps haven't been around that long, so how did people meet before throughout human history? Well, in person. You have to meet people in real life. Meeting a potential lover in real life is much better than meeting them online; you get to feel their personality, energy, and how they carry themselves. That person gets a feeling of you as well.

You can cut many of these messaging games if you create a good first impression. If you meet a girl in person and ask for her number correctly, when you text her, she may show interest immediately, and be easier than building investment from a random girl online from a dating app who never met you. You must optimize to increase your social skills and put yourself out there more. There are different things you can do and places you can go, such as online meetups. If you go to websites like meetup.com or event.com, you can take advantage of meetups for singles. There are many places and things you can do here, to name a few:

- Networking events
- Group gatherings
- Dog parks
- Going out more
- Gyms
- Volunteer groups

I know it can be hard to put yourself out there, but understand that dating in this date and age is not easy for anyone. Dating apps and social media may had good intentions. I am sure they wanted to make it easier for people to connect, get to know each other, and build relationships, but arguably, they have done the opposite; for some reason, our connected world has disconnected us more than ever before. American psychiatrist Edward Hallowell says, "Never in human history have our brains had to work with as much information as they do today We have a generation of people who are so busy processing the information received from all directions that they are losing the ability to think and feel.' that means that the technology that was supposed to help us be more connected and bring us together is having the opposite effect.

The high increase in connections seems to result in a parallel increase in disconnection. You have to do what you can, and it may be harder, or you can say it is different, but meaningful relationships are there for you. Keep doing your best to put yourself out there, and don't feel bad about taking a break from dating if you need it. Sometimes things come when you are not looking for them.

CONCLUSION

Texting a woman in a way that brings success is an art that will take time to develop. We, as guys, struggle with this because we go with our instincts. We think more with our dicks than with our brains with women. It is natural to go aggressively after a woman we are interested in. But when it comes to dating, we need to think and act more objectively and less instinctively. If we can do that, our success with women will increase. Self-awareness, knowledge, the right action, and patience will pay off. And don't worry, you will make mistakes along the way, it is not about perfection. It is about progress. Do not underestimate the importance of self-awareness.

Knowing yourself and why you are struggling gives you the clarity to understand your situation and if you combine that with the knowledge that this book has given you and action, your situation can only improve. It is sad to see so many men that are lonely and depressed because they don't have success with women in their lives. You need to be your relationships' leader and your own life's CEO. You probably wish things were simpler like they used to be and that you did not have to play all these games to get attention sex or the relationship you want from women.

Modern dating has done this, and that is all we have now; the only thing you can do is learn how to navigate this new dating world. The best advice I can give you is to be in your purpose, have your own life, and work on your goals, dreams, and what you want out of life. Be a lifelong learner, always be in an ongoing situation of learning to better yourself, whether it is with women, work, social skills, career or whatever skill you want to improve whenever, wherever, and however. Your competence will become your confidence. Be always on the ongoing education of the self. Once you do this, it will be easier for you to progress in every area of life, not only with women. One of the most important things to keep in mind when dating and texting women is the importance of focusing on yourself and your goals. By doing this, you'll be able to attract women drawn to confident, driven individuals. Additionally, focusing on yourself and your purpose will help ensure that you don't become too fixated on any one woman, which can lead to frustration and disappointment. Instead, you'll be able to approach dating and texting with a sense of abundance and confidence, which can be highly attractive to potential partners.

I hope this book has helped you text women more effectively and given you a perspective of where we are in this world of modern dating. Many men do not stop thinking about why we are struggling so much with women in this date and age. The good thing is that many things are within your control. I hope this book gave you a good perspective and the foundations to help you improve your relationships with women by texting them more effectively.

Thank you for reading our book! We hope you found it informative, interesting, and enjoyable. If you have benefited from reading our book, we would greatly appreciate it if you could leave a review. By leaving a review, you will help other readers discover our book and benefit from it. I would love to know in the reviews how this book has helped you and what you think it overall if there is something I missed or something you would have liked to learn so other people can get your insights. Awareness brings knowledge, and knowledge with action brings change. And I hope this book has helped you achieve precisely that. Thank you again for your support, and we hope that you continue to enjoy reading our work

RESOURCES

https://thesocialman.com/how-to-get-a-girl-to-like-you/

https://thoughtcatalog.com/azelle-lee/2016/02/this-is-whats-going-through-her-mind-when-you-dont-text-her-back/

https://www.scienceofpeople.com/clingy/

https://medium.com/moments-of-passion/how-to-be-persistent-without-being-needy-d44dd33f8d72

https://www.sciencedaily.com/releases/2011/02/110207142623.htm#:~:text=for%20Valentine's%20Day%3F-,Here's%20some%20dating%20advice%20straight%20from%20the%20laboratory%3A%20It%20turns,how%20much%20he%20likes%20her.

https://www.joe.ie/life-style/amount-men-30-not-sex-nearly-tripled-past-decade-663846

https://workretiredie.com/2021/04/22/the-rise-in-male-virginity-explained/

https://www.wikihow.com/Text-a-Girl-That-You-Like

https://www.nicknotas.com/blog/8-basic-rules-for-texting-a-girl-you-like/

www.ingramcontent.com/pod-product-compliance
Lightning Source LLC
Chambersburg PA
CBHW051841130726
47987CB00002B/643